Title page from Revenue Marine Journal
National Archives

THE UNITED STATES REVENUE CUTTERS IN THE CIVIL WAR

By FLORENCE KERN

A U.S. COAST GUARD BICENTENNIAL PUBLICATION

By the same author

Hopley Yeaton's U. S. Revenue Cutter SCAMMEL 1791-1798
John Foster Williams' U. S. Revenue Cutter MASSACHUSETTS 1791-1792
Jonathan Maltbie's U.S. Revenue Cutter ARGUS 1791-1804
Patrick Dennis' U. S. Revenue Cutter VIGILANT 1791-1798
James Montgomery's U. S. Revenue Cutter GENERAL GREEN 1791-1797
Simon Gross's U. S. Revenue Cutter ACTIVE 1791-1798
Richard Taylor's U. S. Revenue Cutter VIRGINIA 1791-1797
William Cooke's U. S. Revenue Cutter DILIGENCE 1792-1798
Robert Cochrane's U. S. Revenue Cutter SOUTH CAROLINA 1793-1798
John Howell's U.S. Revenue Cutter EAGLE 1793-1799
Transcribed Journal of MASSACHUSETTS
Transcribed Journal of ARGUS
Biography of Captain Elisha Hinman
Captain William Cooke Pease, Coast Guard Pioneer

Alised Enterprises
7808 Maryknoll Avenue
Bethesda, Maryland

Foreword

The United States Coast Guard is very fortunate to have Florence Kern devote her considerable talents to presenting its history. The Service has learned much concerning its early years through her writings. Mrs. Kern is a foremost scholar of the early years of the cutter service and this work adds to her already substantial reputation. She points with great pride to the fact that she studied under the late Howard Chapelle. And, I am sure, he would take the same pride in her numerous accomplishments.

Robert L. Scheina
Historian, U.S. Coast Guard

"Nor must Uncle Sam's Web-feet be forgotten. At all the watery margins they have been present. Not only on the deep sea, the broad bay and the rapid river, but also up the narrow, muddy bayou, and wherever the ground was a little damp, they have been and made their tracks."

PRESIDENT ABRAHAM LINCOLN
August 26, 1863

TO ALL THE LIEUTENANTS

OF THE

UNITED STATES REVENUE MARINE SERVICE

WHO KEPT THE LOGS (JOURNALS)

OF THE

REVENUE CUTTERS IN THE CIVIL WAR

AND TO

TERRY MATCHETTE, WILLIAM SHERMAN, CYNTHIA GHEE,

GEORGE BRISCOE AND ALL THE OTHER ARCHIVISTS AT

THE NATIONAL ARCHIVES WHO HELPED ME RESEARCH THEM.

Preface

Scholars in American history have tended to slight the importance of the United States Coast Guard in the growth of the nation. This is particularly true of the Civil War period even though President Lincoln himself depended on the Revenue Marine Service, forerunner of the Coast Guard, not only to protect the revenue, as usual, but to assist in the blockade, guard harbors East and West, and fight off Confederate privateers. Little recognition has been given to the war efforts of the 219 Revenue Marine officers on 57 revenue cutters who not only carried on their many peacetime duties but worked with the Army, Navy, Marines and Coast Survey to bring the tragic war to its conclusion.

In Record Group 26, at the National Archives in Washington, District of Columbia, are numerous documents for this four-year period. They include abstracts and transcripts of the journals of the cutters (sometimes called "logs"), some of the journals themselves, and hundreds of letters to and from officers in the Revenue Marine Service, and in the subsequent (after 1863) Revenue Cutter Service, There are also Treasury Department records, records of applications for commissions, letters to and from Collectors at all the ports in the United States, career resumes, and descriptions of many of the cutters. Some seem not to have been read since being placed in the government files well over 100 years ago. Although kept under archival conditions, the documents are so numerous that they are crowded in cardboard boxes. Many had been sewn together with thread and then folded in three and tied with archival tape. In some cases the thread and tape have disintegrated, and the paper is so brittle it breaks where folded. Much of the ink has faded, and a number of the documents are now illegible. Documents bound in leather volumes are more readable, but the bindings themselves have crumbled with age, and, in some cases, are loose or missing.

It would seem that the time has come to study Record Group 26 and to evaluate the contents of these valuable documents before their message is lost. My two-year study is only a beginning.

Contents

CHAPTER I

On the Eve of Secession

The year 1860 found the United States Revenue Marine Service at low ebb. There were only 24 revenue cutters to police and guard a coastline that extended from the Atlantic Ocean at Eastport, Maine, to the Gulf of Mexico, and up the Pacific Coast from San Diego to Port Townsend, Washington Territory.

Twenty-three were wooden sailing vessels built for the Revenue Marine in the burgeoning age of steam. Of these, one had been launched in 1832, one in 1837, one in 1842, three in 1849, six in 1853, one in 1855, two in 1856, and seven in 1857. One was a former pilot boat, purchased in 1855. They ranged in length from 35 to 100 feet. One was a brig; the rest were fore-and-aft or topsail schooners. The only modern cutter in the fleet was the *Harriet Lane*, a 180-foot wooden side-wheel steamer built in 1857-1858 at the insistence of New York shipping interests. She was the pride of the nation.

Except for the *Harriet Lane*, which was well staffed, the cutters lacked sufficient officers and crew to carry out the work assigned to them. Many had only one or two officers and crews of six or seven, making it difficult to send officers and crew off in small boats to board and examine maritime traffic and to seize law-breakers. There had been drastic cutbacks in the personnel in the 1840's and 1850's, and no pay increases. As a result the service had lost some of its most able men, including Captains John McGowan, Alexander V. Fraser, and William A. Howard.

Earlier Days in the Revenue Marine

Designed by Secretary of the Treasury Alexander Hamilton in 1789-1790 and established by an Act of Congress August 4, 1790, the service had no official name until 1863. In the interim it was called, unofficially, a system of boats, a system of cutters, the Revenue-Marine, the United States Revenue Service and the United States Revenue Marine Service. It was President Lincoln who called it the "Revenue Cutter Service" shortly before it was officially referred to as the "United States Revenue-Cutter Service" by Congress in 12. Stat. 639, February 4, 1863. In part the Statute read:

> An Act in Relation to Commissioned Officers of the United States Revenue Cutter Service
>
> Be it enacted by the State and House of Representatives of the United States of America in Congress assembled That the commissioned officers of the United States revenue cutter service shall be appointed by the President, by and with the advice and consent of the Senate.[1]

Not until January 28, 1915, when the service merged with the Life-Saving Service, was the name changed to "United States Coast Guard." Prior to this, the name "coast guard" had been applied to a number of local organizations. There was a "Coast Guard Committee" at New Bedford, Massachusetts, during the Civil War,[2] and "a Union Coast Guard"[3] as part of the Union forces fighting in North Carolina, also in the Civil War. The Confederates also had a "coast guard."[4] In his annual report to the Treasury Department in 1846, Captain Alexander Fraser spoke of the service as "a coast guard in time of war."[5]

Hamilton's original "system of cutters" was a loosely organized fleet of ten vessels, built and placed in service several years before the United States Navy, to patrol and police the United States coastline from the boundary at Eastport, Maine, to the boundary at St. Mary's, Georgia. At each of the ten leading ports on the coast, a small schooner or sloop was built under local supervision to enforce the new nation's revenue and navigation laws. These were used to board and examine all incoming vessels. In the beginning they were armed only with muskets, pistols, bayonets and a few old guns, relics of the American Revolution. Officers and men had no prescribed uniforms and were called "masters" and "mates." Each vessel was assigned one master, one mate and about ten "people" (crew). There was no insignia.

Their duties were primarily aimed at reducing smuggling and encouraging American shipping and shipbuilding, but gradually other responsibilities were assigned by the Collectors in the districts they patrolled. In some instances, they were used to service lighthouses and other aids to navigation, conduct fishery patrols, work with quarantine stations, draw charts and write sailing directions, and, in districts where the slave trade was outlawed, detain slave ships. Officers were not detailed to assist vessels in distress but often answered calls for help, not only from shipwrecked sailors but from vessels with mutinies on board. With the establishment of the United States Navy in 1798, military duties were assigned. On March 2, 1799, Congress ordered the cutters to operate with the Navy, at the President's discretion, in time of trouble. At the same time uniforms were designed for the officers (by the Navy) and officers were allowed to use naval titles. An ensign with vertical stripes was designed.

The service grew slowly during the first half of the 19th century but proved its worth, not only in the economic development of the nation but in the French-American Quasi War, the War of 1812, the skirmishes with Indians in Florida and on Puget Sound, the Mexican-American War, the Nullification Difficulties, the expedition to Paraguay, and in the constant hunt for pirates, plunderers, wreckers and slavers.

As the nation expanded, cutters were assigned to new ports — St. Augustine, Key West, Pensacola, Mobile, New Orleans, San Francisco, Astoria, Oregon Territory, and Port Townsend, Washington Territory. They took with them the laws of the land as well as the laws of the sea, and became a safety net around the whole nation. The network was complete and intact for just 11 years before it was totally disrupted by the Secessionists in the South.

Although Hamilton had hoped that the cutters would eventually answer only to Federal authority, the Customs Collectors took more and more control of the service. Politics entered the picture early. Officers were chosen not on a merit system, but by political appointment. There was no uniform management until 1843 when a central bureau was established and the knowledgeable Captain Alexander Fraser was made Bureau Chief.[6] In the regulations he issued in 1843, the collectors' authority was diminished, and cutter captains were ordered to make monthly reports to the Bureau.[7] He established a merit system of promotion, and by rotating officers from vessel to vessel, undermined the power of local politicians. He prohibited slavery on the cutters and improved the life of the "people" by increasing their pay and prohibiting flogging and other brutalities. These and other reforms he accomplished in his short time as Chief, and while the nation was at war with Mexico.

He left the Bureau in 1848. A year later the office itself was abolished. Collectors once more began to take control. From 1848 to 1860 many of the old practices and policies were back in full swing.[8]

During the 1840's the service faced a major problem when it attempted to switch from sail to steam. In this too, Fraser was influential. When steam fever reached the Revenue Marine Service, Fraser advocated the building of paddle-wheelers. Instead, six experimental propeller and horizontal-wheel steamers were built at a cost of $620,000. For one reason or another, all were failures. Even two paddle-wheelers proved ineffective. One, the *Polk*, eventually had its paddle wheels and engine removed, and carried on under sail alone. Some of the other steamers became lightships, or were turned over to the Coast Survey, or abandoned. It was an unhappy era for the Revenue Marine.

As a result, the service was more or less neglected in the 1850s. Twenty cutters were built between 1849 and 1859 but they were all wooden sailing vessels. It was not until *Harriet Lane* went down the ways in 1858 that another steam vessel joined the service.

In the 1840-1860 period, additional duties were assigned to the cutters, including winter cruising off the coast for the protection of mariners.[9] They were also ordered to enforce immigration laws.[10] This was of major importance on the West Coast where Chinese coolie labor meant overcrowded vessels. The immigration laws were explicit about the steerage passengers between the United States and Europe, or ports on the Pacific. The number of passengers was limited to "one for every 14 clear superficial feet of the lower deck, not occupied by ship's stores or cargo, where the height between decks exceeds six feet." Children were not counted. Short persons were allowed less room. Deck houses with windows and doors were required, and every vessel carrying more than 50 persons was required to have a "camboose" (stove) for their use. For each person on an Atlantic voyage it was ordered that "60 gallons of water, 100 pounds of salted beef, 100 pounds of wholesome ship bread, and one gallon of vinegar" be provided. The master was also required to provide a "water closet or privy for every 100 passengers, under a penalty of 50 dollars."

In addition to all these duties, cutter officers had to be "semper paratus" to receive on board and entertain domestic and foreign dignitaries. Even George Washington had enjoyed outings on the cutters. He had fished from the decks of *Scammel* in Portsmouth, New Hampshire, and *Vigilant* in New York Harbor. *Harriet Lane* was hardly afloat before she was visited at the Brooklyn Navy Yard by two Russian diplomats, and Mohammed Pasha, youngest admiral in the Turkish Navy. They were taken on a cruise down New York Harbor to Coney Island.[11]

Some of the collectors entertained so frequently — and so lavishly — on the cutters in the 1850s that the press called the service a "pleasure fleet."[12] There was public pressure to abolish it altogether, or transfer it to the Navy.

War in the Offing

With war on the horizon in December 1860, Secretary of the Treasury Howell Cobb voiced his opinions on the Revenue Service as follows in his annual report to Congress:

> In this connection [revenue laws] the attention of Congress is called to the condition of the revenue marine service. With the exception of the Harriet Lane, there are none but sail vessels employed in the service. Steam vessels are so rapidly supplanting sail vessels in the commercial service that the present sail vessels of the revenue service however well adapted to a former state of things are becoming almost useless for the purpose for which they are employed. I have before represented to the Congress that this service could be transferred to the Navy Department with benefit to the public interest and I entertain the same opinion now.[13]

Cobb recommended that in the meantime steam vessels should be substituted for the sailing cutters, that the officer corps be maintained, and the pay increased. He found the pay did not correspond with the compensation of officers employed in "similar and less laborious duties." He felt pay should be raised as "an act of simple justice to a worthy class of public officers."[14]

Before Congress could consider his proposals, the country was in a state of upheaval. Cobb himself fled Washington to join his friends in the South, and flags of secession were flying in six of the southern ports in which Revenue Cutters were stationed. The fate of the nation, as well as of the Revenue Marine Service, was in the balance.

Abraham Lincoln

CHAPTER II

Revenue Cutters of 1860

On December 17, 1860, the revenue cutters in the United States Revenue Marine Service were:

Andrew Jackson at Eastport, Maine
Caleb Cushing at Portland, Maine
Morris at Boston, Massachusetts
James Campbell at New London, Connecticut
Harriet Lane at New York, New York
Walter B. Forward at Wilmington, Delaware
Philip Allen at Baltimore, Maryland
William J. Duane at Norfolk, Virginia
William Aiken at Charleston, South Carolina
James C. Dobbin at Savannah, Georgia
John Appleton at Key West, Florida
Lewis Cass at Mobile, Alabama
Robert McClelland at New Orleans, Louisiana
Washington at New Orleans, Louisiana
Henry Dodge at Galveston, Texas
William L. Marcy at San Francisco, California
Joseph Lane at Astoria, Oregon Territory
Jefferson Davis at Port Townsend, Washington Territory
Howell Cobb at Oswego, New York
Jeremiah S. Black at Erie, Pennsylvania
Jacob Thompson at Detroit, Michigan
Aaron V. Brown at Milwaukee, Wisconsin
Isaac Toucey at Michilimackinac, Michigan
John B. Floyd at Marquette, Michigan[1]

Perhaps nowhere on the continent were the issues of the times more hotly contested than on board the cutters. Almost as many officers were from the South as from the North. All had taken the double pledge of allegiance, first to uphold and defend the Constitution of the United States, second to obey the laws of the Revenue Marine Service. United, many of them for years, against foreign law-breakers, their ranks were now divided. In cabins and ward rooms in all the major ports of the United States, Southern officers argued for the South, Northerners for the North.

The *Andrew Jackson* at Eastport

The cutter *Andrew Jackson*, a schooner, was the oldest in the fleet. She had been built about 1832 at the Washington Navy Yard, and named for the seventh President of the United States. Most of her early life was spent in the South. In 1833 she was one of five cutters sent to Charleston under command of Captain William A. Howard to enforce the revenue laws when South Carolina threatened to nullify the Constitution. A few years later she took part in the Seminole War. She also fought pirates off Florida.[2]

For 17 years she went North only for repairs but in 1855 she was ordered to Eastport, Maine, on the Canadian border. Here she hunted smugglers, enforced fishing laws, serviced lighthouses, and rescued friend and foe alike when in distress on the rocky coast.[3] She was stationed in Whale Cove.

Her commander in 1860 was the veteran Captain John S. Prouty. There were 11 men in the crew. When the fateful year 1861 began, Captain Prouty had just died and Lieutenant Amasa Hyde was in command. He began *Jackson's* journal for 1861 by writing:

"A Happy New Year to all."[4]

The *Caleb Cushing* at Portland

The *Caleb Cushing* was one of six handsome schooners launched the same week in July 1853 at the two shipyards of J. M. Hood. One yard was in Bristol, Rhode Island, the other in nearby Somerset, Massachusetts. Four of the schooners including *Cushing* were fore-and-aft rigged; two were top-sail rigged. *Cushing* was built at the Somerset yard under the supervision of Revenue Cutter Captain Napoleon L. Coste.[5] She was named for a New England politician and statesman who served in Congress and was later Attorney General. In 1860 Cushing believed it was more important to save the Union than to abolish slavery.

The *Cushing* spent most of her lifetime in Maine. In 1860 she was boarding and examining as many as 30 cargo and fishing vessels a day, assisting in the service of lighthouses, putting down mutinies aboard vessels in Portland, and answering other distress calls. There were other ports of importance in Maine - Bath, Castine, Machias, Kittery, Bangor - but these had only small revenue boats for harbor work. The *Cushing* handled all the important assignments. In 1860 there was no cutter stationed between Portland and Boston. Portsmouth, which had been an important port when the service was instituted in 1790 and had maintained one of the first cutters, the *Scammel*, now had only harbor boats.

Captain Green Walden, a veteran of the service, had commanded *Cushing* since she was launched, but in November 1860 his health failed and he asked permission to remain at his home on Cape Elizabeth, Maine. Command of the cutter went to another old-timer, First Lieutenant Joseph Amazeen, in December.[6]

The *Morris* at Boston

The *Morris* was launched in 1849 at John Brown's shipyard in Baltimore, with Revenue Cutter Captain John M. Jones supervising her construction. She was one of four topsail schooner cutters built that year.[7] Named for the Revolutionary War financier and statesman, Robert Morris, she replaced an earlier *Morris* lost in a Key West hurricane in 1846.

She had been stationed at Boston since 1853. In 1854 she participated in two dramatic events, one the search for the missing steamer the *San Francisco*,[8] and the other, the return of fugitive slave, Anthony Burns, from Boston to his owner in Norfolk, Virginia.[9] Her cruising grounds were from Portsmouth, New Hampshire, to New Bedford in Southern Massachusetts. When not off cruising she could usually be found at Central Wharf, Boston. In 1860, she was doing extensive cruising, boarding between eight and ten cargo and fishing vessels a day, as well as visiting lighthouses in the district and responding to calls for help. Many of the vessels boarded came from the South with cotton and rice, returning with ice and lumber.[10]

The *James Campbell* at New London

The *James Campbell* was one of the six schooners launched the same week in 1853 at the shipyards of J. M. Hood. She was built at the Somerset, Massachusetts, yard under the supervision of Captain Coste, and was especially designed for the New London district to service the eastern end of Long Island Sound, Buzzards Bay, Block Island Sound, and Vineyard Sound.[11]

There has always been confusion in Coast Guard records over the name "*Campbell*," for there were three early *Campbells* — all named for George Washington Campbell, Secretary of the Treasury under President Madison. The name of the third *Campbell* was changed in 1855 to *Joseph Lane*. The fourth "*Campbell*" was named for James Campbell who was Attorney General and, in 1860, Postmaster General.

In 1860, the *James Campbell* made daily cruises within range of New London, and once a month took a week's cruise to Buzzards Bay and Vineyard Sound, boarding dozens of vessels at such favorite anchorages as Tarpaulin Cove on the Elizabeth Islands, and Holmes Hole on Martha's Vineyard. Her commander was Captain George Clarke. In November 1860, she assisted a vessel in distress off Cuttyhunk.[12]

The *Harriet Lane* at New York

Harriet Lane, showcase of the fleet, was stationed at the Battery off the lower end of Manhattan in 1860. She had been launched nearby, at the yard of William Webb on the East River, in February 1858. She cost $140,000. Designed by Naval Constructor Samuel Pook, and supervised and command- ed by Revenue Cutter Captain John Faunce,[13] she was a 674 13/95 ton paddle- wheel steam cutter, measuring 180 feet, with a 30-foot beam, a 12 1/2 foot depth, and a draft of ten feet. Like all the other early steam vessels, she car- ried auxiliary sail. She was brig-rigged. Her paddle wheels spun at 20 rpm, her boiler pressure was about 25 pounds and she could make 12 knots under steam.[14] William Dunham was her first chief engineer.

She and the subsequent *Harriet Lanes* were the only cutters named for a woman, the woman being Miss Harriet Lane, niece of President James Buchanan, and hostess in the White House at the time the cutter was launched.[15]

The cutter made a trial run under steam March 1, 1858 when she "stood up the river off the Novelty Works, rounded up and stood back." She then went as far as Sandy Hook Lightship, returning at noon to the dock at the foot of 7th Street in the East River. The next few days were spent adjusting her engine, taking on one 32-pounder gun, one 12-pounder Howitzer, small arms and rations, and bending on her sails. On March 11 she "got up steam" and went to the Brooklyn Navy Yard across the river where her first cele- brity visitor,[8] Admiral Mohammed Pasha of Turkey, and two officers of the Russian Navy came aboard for a cruise to Coney Island.[16]

Two 24-pounder Howitzers were added before she was sent to cruise the coast in search of slavers. In July 1858 she was taken into the Navy, with her Revenue Marine officers and crew on board, to join an expedition to Paraguay, South America, to settle an international dispute. Returned to the Revenue Marine in 1859, she went on a cruise to New London, and then to Cape May, searching for vessels suspected of slaving. She also entertained many celebrities, chief among them the glamorous Harriet Lane.[17]

Her officers at this time included four second lieutenants, Henry O. Porter, Daniel D. Tompkins, R. T. Travis and D. C. Constable, and two third lieutenants, T. M. Dungan and Charles R. Berrett, in addition to the engineers. Other officers in the 1858-1860 period included First Lieutenants A. D. Stanford and George R. Slicer, and Third Lieutenants I. H. Thatcher and H. J. Gambrill. She had about 50 men in her crew.

After cruising around New York in search of suspected slavers and fillibusterers, she was ordered South in late 1859. She spent the winter off the Carolinas and Florida where she worked with the local customs collectors in boarding vessels suspected of smuggling and/or slave running. She became well acquainted with the waters of Charleston and Savannah.

In May 1860 she returned to New York where efforts were being made to seize the slave ship *Kate. Kate* was boarded after a chase about five miles outside Sandy Hook, and brought back to the Battery. On June 28, 1860, the New York Customs Collector and several Treasury Department officials came on board to go down the harbor and salute the incoming British steamer *Great Eastern* which had broken the transatlantic speed record. The very next day *Harriet Lane* was hostess to 80 citizens of Japan, the first official delegation from Japan to visit the United States.

In August, still pursuing suspected slaveships, the *Harriet Lane* cruised to southern New England, passing Fire Island, Montauk and Cuttyhunk, and anchoring off Gay Head Light House, where two government agents went ashore to confer with the lighthouse keeper about suspected vessels. Returning to New York she was severely damaged in a collision with a schooner in Hell Gate. Repairs took the last week in August but by September she was chasing *Kate* again. *Kate* had escaped but was later seized as she left for the coast of *Africa*.

In October the cutter was ordered to Washington, where on October 5, she was hostess to President Buchanan, his 29-year old niece, Harriet, and His Royal Highness, 19-year old Edward, Prince of Wales (later Edward 7th), visiting under the soubriquet "Lord Renfrew." On October 6 they cruised to Aquia Creek where Harriet Lane and the Prince witnessed a slave auction. The Prince then "took the cars" for a land tour. The cutter returned to New York and met him at the railroad terminal at Perth Amboy. After a cruise to West Point, the Prince, by then highly popular with officers and crew, left for England presenting $800 to the crew and a handsome gold watch to Captain Faunce. Faunce received special permission from headquarters to keep the watch.[18] One wonders where it is now.

A few days after the Prince departed, Secretary of the Treasury Howell Cobb and other Washington dignitaries came on board to cruise up the North River and down the Bay. Two days later Faunce was ordered to seize the propeller steamer *Victoria* suspected of slaving. In November she seized the schooner *W. L. Cogswell* near Bedloes Island (then devoid of any statues). In December 1860 the crew began shovelling snow from the decks.[19]

The *Walter B. Forward* at Wilmington, Delaware

Third oldest cutter in the 1860 fleet was the *Walter B. Forward*, built at William Easby's shipyard in Georgetown (now the site of the Kennedy Center), District of Columbia, in 1842[20] and named for the then Secretary of the Treasury. She was a 139 13/95 ton schooner, 90 feet long, with a beam of 21 feet 2 inches. Built of oak and locust, with copper and iron fastenings, her mainmast was 63 feet above the hull with the topmast adding another 33 feet 3 inches. Her main boom was 51 feet 8 inches long, her foreyard 53 feet and her topsail yards 33 feet 5 inches. Her bowsprit extended outboard 19 feet. Her rigging was of 4-inch Russian hemp.

There were 6 berths in the ward room and main cabin. Furnishings included 6 hair mattresses, 6 stone wash basins, Queensware cups and saucers, 17 bound books, 8 tablecloths, 1 looking glass, 1 artificial horizon and a cabin stove and pipes. She cost $3,786.75 and was built under the supervision of Captain Henry Prince.[21]

The *Forward* had played a major part in assisting the Navy in the War with Mexico in 1846. She was transferred briefly to the Coast Survey in 1847 and, in 1854, was sent to search for the missing steamer *San Francisco*.[22]

In 1860, under the command of Captain Henry G. Nones she patrolled Delaware River and Bay from Philadelphia to the Delaware Breakwater. In December she went aground in a gale in Christmas Creek, Newcastle, Delaware.[23]

The *Philip Allen* at Baltimore

The *Philip Allen*, a schooner, was built by Page and Allen at Portsmouth, Virginia, in 1855,[24] and was named for Senator Allen, a leader in the Democratic party, Governor of Rhode Island, cotton manufacturer and builder of the first steam engine in Rhode Island. He was known as a "Tariff Democrat."

Allen, stationed at Baltimore, patrolled the upper Chesapeake Bay and its many tributaries. She normally carried three officers and a crew of ten. In December 1860 her officers were Captain Thomas Sands, an officer since 1833, and Lieutenants R. A. Morsell and Charles R. Berret.

Much of the international and coastwise traffic that came into Baltimore had already been boarded and inspected at Norfolk. *Allen's* chief duties involved inspecting outward bound vessels and the almost limitless number of log canoes, bugeyes, and pungies that criss-crossed the Bay carrying fish, oysters, produce and lumber. On December 11, 1860, she boarded 18 of them at Drum Point on the Paxtuxent River. The same day she inspected an abandonned American schooner at Point Lookout. Her crew was treated to a rare sight August 5 at Annapolis. As recorded in her Journal:

> At 5 PM the steamship *"Great Eastern"* anchored in Annapolis Roads. His Excellency, the President of the United States [Buchanan] passed out of the harbor on U.S. Steam Vessel *Anacostia* to visit the steam ship *Great Eastern*.[25]

Philip Allen fired a 21-gun for the President as he passed by.

The *William J. Duane* at Norfolk

Built in the Philadelphia shipyard of Jacob Tees in 1848-1849, under the supervision of Revenue Cutter Lieutenant John McGowan,[26] the *William J. Duane* was named for the man who had been Secretary of the Treasury under President Jackson. She was one of four topsail schooners measuring between 150 and 155 tons built that year. She carried a crew of fifteen.

Much of her early life was spent in New Orleans but in 1855 she was ordered to Norfolk where she boarded and inspected hundreds of vessels at the entrance to Chesapeake Bay. They carried cargo that ranged from yokes of oxen brought down from Maine, to oranges, lemons and brimstone from Sicily. Some were found to have contraband "seegars" from Havana on board. She aided many vessels in distress, and regularly visited the district's lightships, leaving men to tend the lights while the lightship keepers had time off.

Duane was commanded in 1860 by Captain Richard Evans, one of the oldest officers in the service, and a Southern sympathizer. Snow and hail plagued Norfolk in December. There was much unrest along the waterfront.[27]

The *William Aiken* at Charleston

In 1855 a former Charleston pilot schooner named *Eclipse* was purchased from ship chandler Hugh Vincent by the U.S. Treasury Department for $4,500.[28] She became the Revenue Cutter *William Aiken*, named for the wealthy southern planter whose great rice plantation at Jehossee Island near Charleston was a model of agriculture. Aiken, of Irish descent, had been Governor of South Carolina, and was widely known as a statesman and philanthropist.

The cutter's cruising grounds included the seacoast from North Carolina to St. Mary's, Florida. She carried a crew of twelve. She was armed with six muskets and six cutlasses, and was no match for the buccaneers and slave traders who abounded in the waters she patrolled. She was commanded by Captain Coste, who had fought aboard the steam cutter *Legare* in the War with Mexico, and had supervised the building of four cutters at Somerset, Massachusetts in 1853.[29]

Although ordered to enforce the law and seize slave ships, Coste evaded the issue. By 1860, he was in open defiance of government regulations. In December 1859 he wrote in *Aiken's* Journal:

> Boarded and examined Schr *William & John* of Charleston from St. Thomas, Captain Paris, with 250 negroes bought by B. Boyle, Esq. to be carried to Montgomery, Alabama.[30]

The *James C. Dobbin* at Savannah

The *James C. Dobbin* was another of the six schooners launched at the J. M. Hood shipyards in July 1853, and one of the four supervised by Captain Coste.[31] Her name, surely an odd one for a cutter, derived from James Cochran Dobbin, Secretary of the Navy under President Franklin Pierce in 1853. Dobbin knew little about the sea or the Navy but became popular with Navy men when he favored the building of steam vessels and increased the size of the service. The cutter *Dobbin* carried a crew of fourteen.

In 1854 *Dobbin* was one of the cutters sent in search of the missing steamer *San Francisco*. After serving in Wilmington, Delaware, she was ordered to Savannah under the command of the highly popular Captain Robert Day, a native of Savannah, who had fought on the steam cutter *Legare* in the War with Mexico. *Dobbin* did little or nothing to eliminate the slave trade when under his command.

Captain Day died July 22, 1860. Command then went to the Yankee Captain John A. Webster Jr., whose father had been a popular commander in the service. Serving with him were two avowed Southerners, Lieutenants Alex R. Abercrombie and John G. Blackwood. Webster was granted a month's leave in November but was back on board *Dobbin* when South Carolina declared her independence December 20.[32]

The *John Appleton* at Key West

The *John Appleton* was the smallest cutter in the fleet in 1860. She was a 35-ton schooner built at Page and Allen's shipyard in Portsmouth, Virginia, in 1857, and sent to Key West under the command of Lieutenant William B. Randolph. She was expected to patrol the east and west coasts of Florida.[33]

Lieutenant Randolph had no junior officers and very few in crew. Allowed $20 a month for a cook, he could find no one willing to take the job so he implored the Secretary of the Treasury to let him use his own slave, then working as a laborer on a Key West fort at $30 a month. No slaves were permitted on board the cutters in 1860. Randolph's grievances were many. He did not know how he could be expected to look for "supposed slavers, and vessels in distress, at sea, in all kinds of weather, cruising in a little vessel that one can scarcely turn around in."[34]

Early in 1861, *Appleton* was turned over to the Navy.

The *Lewis Cass* at Mobile

The *Lewis Cass*, a schooner, was built in 1855 at Page and Allen's shipyard in Portsmouth, Virginia, under the supervision of Revenue Cutter Captain Robert K. Hudgins.[35] She was expressly designed for service in New Orleans and was named for Lewis Cass of Exeter, New Hampshire, who ran for President on the Democratic ticket in 1848 and was later Secretary of State under President Buchanan. On December 12, 1860, he resigned because troops had not been sent to reinforce Major Anderson at Fort Sumter.

The cutter *Cass* remained in New Orleans under command of John G. Breshwood until July 1860, when she was ordered to Mobile. Breshwood, an able commander, kept an excellent journal. His daily reports tell of ordering the masters of slave ships to report to the New Orleans Collectors but there, apparently, the matter ended. As late as September 1860, when he was stationed in Mobile, he had his men remove questionable cargo (trade goods and manacles) from the *Cynget* before she sailed for Africa. He had 13 men in his crew.

In November Captain Breshwood was ordered to the *Robert McClelland* at New Orleans and Captain James J. Morrison took command of the *Cass*. Morrison found the cutter in poor condition. "Pumps going constantly while underway," he wrote in the Journal, "vessel out of trim with too much water in bilge." A few days later he wrote: "Deck leaking badly wetting the bedding in the cabin and ward room." Morrison, like Breshwood, was a Southerner but his young Lieutenants Charles G. Shoemaker, Thomas H. Lawrence, and Anson F. Rogers were from the North.

By December the cutter was in very bad shape. Even the ensign was so worn out that they had to make a new one out of a bed sheet. Still they continued to patrol. On New Year's Eve 1860 they were underway at nine in the morning and off Red Bluff at ten.[36]

The *Robert McClelland* at New Orleans

One of the six schooners built at the J.M. Hood yards in 1853, the *Robert McClelland* was originally sent to Mobile, Alabama, under command of Captain Douglass Ottinger. Ottinger was just back from San Francisco where he had commanded the cutter *Lawrence* and lost her in a freak accident near the Golden Gate. In 1854 she searched for the missing *San Francisco,* and from 1854 to 1859 spent most of her time cruising in the Gulf of Mexico, boarding and examining vessels off the many mouths of the Mississippi.[37] She was named in honor of the man who had been twice Governor of Michigan and was one of the organizers of the Democratic party. She had 17 men in her crew.

In 1859 she was ordered to New York for repairs. She remained in New York under the command of Captain Robert K. Hudgins until the autumn of 1860 when she was ordered to New Orleans to allow the *Washington* to be taken to New York for repairs. The two cutters exchanged crews off Slaughter House Point, New Orleans, October 13, 1860, Captain Hudgins taking command of *Washington* and Captain Breshwood of *McClelland*.

After the rendez-vous and exchange of officers, Captain Breshwood took the *McClelland* down the river and spent several weeks cruising between Pass a Loutre, Pilots Bay, and Fort Jackson. On board were three ardent Southerners: Breshwood, First Lieutenant Samuel B. Caldwell, and Third Lieutenant Thomas D. Fister. While the cutter was at Fort Jackson, December 29, 1860, Captain Breshwood and Lieutenant Fister left for important business at Mobile. Lieutenant Caldwell, commanding the cutter in their absence, wrote in the Journal that they were to be witnesses for the United States in the District Court.[38]

The *Washington* at New Orleans

Second oldest cutter in the fleet in 1860, and the only sailing brig, was the *Washington*. She had been built as a schooner at Baltimore in 1837 under the supervision of the noted Captain Henry D. Hunter.[39] She was named for the first President and ordered to cruise the Atlantic between New York and Chesapeake Bay. Because she was larger than originally planned, she was found to be too unwieldy as a schooner. In 1838 she was back in Baltimore to be rerigged as a brig.

The late Howard I. Chapelle, in his *History of the American Sailing Navy,* describes her as a "noted sailer" and says her lines reflect "the ideas of Chesapeake Bay builders seeking fast, seagoing vessels." She measured 91 feet 2 inches with a beam of 22 feet 1 inch. Her plans are now in the Smithsonian Museum. She carried a crew of seventeen.[40]

After a brief assignment in the Navy in 1838, the *Washington* was transferred to the Coast Survey in 1840 and remained there until 1852 when she
returned to the Revenue Marine Service and was ordered to Mobile. From
1853 to 1859, she was stationed at New York and was one of the cutters sent
in search of the missing *San Francisco* in 1854, and in search of slaveships in
1858-1859. On June 1, 1859, she was ordered to New Orleans under the command of Captain Hudgins, where she exchanged crews with the cutter
McClelland so that that vessel could be sailed to New York for repairs.

The *Washington's* new commander was Captain James G. Morrison. Her
cruising grounds in 1859-1860 were from Sabine Pass in Texas to Key West
in Florida. She boarded and examined hundreds of vessels. Her journal makes
no mention of slaveships. On one occasion she was sent in pursuit of the
steamer *Propeller* said to be carrying men on a filibustering expedition to seize
land in Mexico. When boarded, Captain Morrison found only law-abiding
citizens and cattle on board.

The cutter obeyed orders from collectors at both Mobile and New Orleans
but received pay and rations from Mobile. On October 13, 1860, she joined
the *McClelland* back from New York and anchored off Slaughter House Point.
The two cutters again exchanged officers and crews. Under command of Captain Hudgins, the *Washington* was then scheduled to sail to New York for
repairs, but on November 27, the order was revoked. Her captain was told
to have the cutter repaired in New Orleans.[41]

The *Henry Dodge* at Galveston

The *Henry Dodge* was one of three topsail schooners built for the Revenue
Marine Service in 1855-1856 by Page and Allen at Portsmouth, Virginia.[42]
She was expressly built for Galveston, Texas. Her sister ships were *Lewis Cass*
and *Philip Allen*. All were supervised by Captain Hudgins during their
construction.

Dodge left Portsmouth for Galveston under command of Lieutenant William
F. Rogers August 1, 1856, arriving September 6. She was named for a fron-
tiersman who had fought in the War of 1812, the Black Hawk War, and the
Winnebago War, and had been Governor of Wisconsin Territory, a United
States Marshal and a United States Senator.

When she reached Galveston, command was given to a crusty old-time
Texan, Levy C. Harby, who had been in and out of the Service since 1829.
Early in his career, his name was stricken from the rolls when he left the cut-
ter *Ingham* to command an armed vessel for the independent State of Texas.
He had been reinstated. He later served aboard cutters in the Seminole War
and in the War with Mexico.[43].

By 1860 he was plagued with rheumatism and spent much time ashore leaving command of the *Dodge* to Lieutenant William F. Rogers. However, he
was on board in March 1860 when the cutter was ordered to report to the
American minister at Vera Cruz for an assignment. En route she was severely

damaged in a gale but was repaired in Vera Cruz by Navy carpenters from the warships *Saratoga* and *Brooklyn*, also there on international business. The *Dodge* carried dispatches from the American minister to Hacienda de Monte Pahio. Upon returning to Vera Cruz, she was delegated to transport a secretary, with dispatches for the Secretary of State, to Galveston.

She made a second trip to Vera Cruz in May and later to Tampico where she anchored close to the Mexican warship *Constitucion* and the American steamer *Ware*. Captain Harby went ashore to visit the American counsel and was presented to Mexican Governor Garcia. He invited them and others to come aboard the *Dodge*. For two days, there were festivities on the cutter with many gun salutes. The weather was "misty and rainy." Towed out to sea by the Mexican *Constitucion*, the *Dodge* carried American diplomats and a large sum of money back to Galveston.[44]

Later an action was brought against Harby by his Second Lieutenant William A. Tennison who accused him of giving rifles to the Mexicans; selling the cutter's sails, two boats and a gig; removing armament; and being abusive to his officers and crew. By then Harby had left the cutter and was ashore suffering from "fever and rheumatism."

When the *Dodge* returned from Mexico, the men went ashore and the cutter was "smoked." When the hatches were opened the next morning, 65 dead rats were removed. The Journal reported no other unusual events until November when two men fell overboard in a gale. Since they could not swim, a boat was lowered to save them.[45]

With Captain Harby ashore, Lieutenant Rogers took command of the cutter. In Washington there were plans to commission him a captain for his long and faithful service, but although the certificate was made out and signed, it never reached him.

The Charleston South Carolina newspaper "Mercury" reported that on Sunday, December 29, not a "single vessel in Galveston flew the United States flag."[46] All that Lieutenant William G. Roche noted that day in the Journal was:

"Commences strong winds from N.E. let go the Starbd anchor and veered away on both chains all hands present served ten rations."[47]

The *Dodge* usually carried a crew of fourteen.

The *William L. Marcy* at San Francisco

In 1860 there were only three Revenue Cutters on the Pacific coast — *William L. Marcy* at San Francisco, *Joseph Lane* at Astoria, Oregon Territory, and *Jefferson Davis* at Port Townsend, Washington Territory. *Marcy* and *Davis* were sister ships, both having been built at J. M. Hood's Bristol, Rhode Island, yard in 1853, and sailed around Cape Horn later that year.[48] They were almost identical. They were topsail schooners 94 feet long, 23 feet wide, with a depth of 9 feet and a tonnage of 179 and a fraction. Both had round sterns, round tucks, carved eagle figureheads, and ornamental shields on their sterns. Each cost approximately $9,000.[49]

The *Marcy* was named for a noted statesman who was Secretary of State in 1852 and the sponsor of the Gadsden Treaty. Mt. Marcy, highest peak in the Adirondacks, was also named in his honor.

The *Marcy* arrived in San Francisco during the height of the Gold Rush and was largely instrumental in establishing American law in an unruly coastal area. Commanded first by Captain Stephen Cornell, she was turned over in March 1858 to Captain William Cooke Pease who had supervised her commissioning five years earlier. He found her in deplorable condition and ordered extensive repairs. Remote from the troubles in the East, the *Marcy*, with 17 men on board, had hundreds of vessels to board and inspect, including an increasing number of over crowded vessels from China. When not cruising, the cutter could often be found at Benicia or at Meigs Wharf in San Francisco. However, by April 1860, wharfage was so expensive in San Francisco that Pease often anchored "out in the stream." He got his water at Sausalito.

By 1860, the *Marcy* was again in need of repairs. Many frames, some outboard planking, 30 feet of her keelson, the bulwarks, the main mast, the main boom, and the windlass were rotten and unsafe. The pumps were too small and much of the copper was worn thin. The estimated cost of repairs was $11,800 — more than it had cost to build her.[50]

Her officers in 1860 were Captain Pease, and Lieutenants J. Harrison Kellogg, J. Edward Wilson and E. Bowling Sturgeon.

The *Joseph Lane* (ex-*Campbell*) at Astoria

Considered one of the fastest and most graceful schooners of the clipper ship days, the *Joseph Lane* was launched July 30, 1849, at the Portsmouth, Virginia, shipyard of Graves and Fenbie.[51] She was originally named *Campbell*. Under that name, she patrolled lower Chesapeake Bay for six years. In 1855 she was ordered to the Pacific to be stationed at Astoria, Oregon Territory, where Joseph Lane was then territorial governor. She was renamed in his honor. The Governor, born in North Carolina, had gone west and had become Superintendent of Indian Affairs. Later, he was an avowed secessionist.

Commanded by Captain John S. S. Chaddock, *Joe Lane*, as she was called, guided vessels over the bar at the entrance to the Columbia River, boarded and examined the increasing number of vessels engaged in lumbering and fishing, visited lighthouses, and assisted mariners caught in the swift currents and ice floes of the river. In 1859 she joined the Navy warship *Massachusetts* in Puget Sound to assist General Winfield Scott in his difficulties with the Indians in that area. She was back in Oregon Territory in December 1860. Captain Chaddock was by then petitioning for an assignment on the Atlantic or on the Great Lakes after 11 years on the Pacific, and his First Lieutenant J. D. Usher was complaining to Secretary Cobb that the Oregon climate was prejudicial to his health. He asked to be transferred East so he could be near his daughter "whose delicate health is a source of great anxiety to me." First

Lieutenant James A. Merryman was willing to stay on board *Joe Lane* when the two other officers left.[52]

The *Jefferson Davis* at Port Townsend

Sister ship of the *William A. Marcy*, the *Jefferson Davis* was named in 1853 in honor of the Southern leader whose name would be anathema in the North during the Civil War.

The *Davis* had sailed to the Pacific around Cape Horn in 1853-1854 under the command of Captain Pease. For several years, she was engaged in skirmishes with Indians in Puget Sound. She was stationed at the thriving port of Port Townsend, not far from Canadian boundaries that were then being disputed. Pease left the cutter to return East in 1856, turning the command over to First Lieutenant James M. Selden who assisted both Army and Navy in continued Indian uprisings.[53]

In 1858 troubles arose between Canada and the United States over San Juan Island in Puget Sound and the *Davis* was ordered to aid in a survey of the island and her principal harbor. She was then under orders from both the Collector at Port Townsend and General Winfield Scott. She was frequently used to carry troops. For a short time she was joined by the *Joe Lane* from Oregon. In December 1860 troubles in the East began to influence relations with Canadians in nearby Victoria, Vancouver Island, and the *Davis* was used to ferry diplomats from the United States to Canada.[54]

The Six Cutters on the Great Lakes

There were six relatively new centerboard cutters on the Great Lakes in December 1860. They had been built under trying circumstances at the yard of Merry and Gay in Milan, Ohio, in 1856-1857, with Captain Pease as superintendent. Each vessel cost $6,500, instead of the $4,050 agreed on in the contract, and many bills had not been paid when the vessels were launched in September 1857. Arguments between the Treasury Department and Ohio financiers led to a seizure of the cutters and a long delay before they were dispersed to their stations. They were all named for Southern men prominent in political life in 1856-1857.

They were not identical but were, on the average, about 63 feet long, 17 feet wide, with a 5 foot draft and a tonnage of 58 74/95. They were handsomely ornamented with eagle figureheads and ornamental shields on their round sterns. In December 1860, the *Howell Cobb* was at Oswego, New York, on Lake Ontario; the *Jeremiah S. Black* at Erie, Pennsylvania, on Lake Erie; the *Jacob Thompson* at Detroit, Michigan, on Lake St. Clair; the *Aaron V. Brown* at Milwaukee, Wisconsin, on Lake Michigan; the *Isaac Toucey* at Michilimackinac, Michigan, on Lake Huron; and the *John B. Floyd* at Marquette, Michigan, on Lake Superior.[55]

All six cutters were laid up for the winter when the lakes froze late in November 1860.

The *Minot* and the *Morgan*

Some Confederate records list two additional cutters in 1860, the *Minot* (renamed *Manasses* by Confederates) at New Bern, North Carolina, and the *Morgan* at Mobile, Alabama. Neither can be found in any official Revenue Marine records. Presumably they were local vessels, not under Federal control.

CHAPTER III

New Flags for Old

On December 17, 1860, South Carolina statesmen in convention at Columbia voted 159 to 0 to secede from the Union. Three days later, the State was "a free and independent nation." Church bells and cannon alike proclaimed the momentous tidings.[1]

Within six weeks, Georgia, Alabama, Florida, Mississippi, Louisiana and Texas had followed South Carolina's example and by February 9, the seven states had formed the Confederate States of America and elected Jefferson Davis as President. All forts and navy yards in the seceding states, except for Fort Sumter at Charleston and Fort Pickens at Pensacola, were seized, and all Federal officials were told to pack up and go North, or better still, join the South.

The *Aiken* Hoists the Palmetto Flag

The United States Revenue Cutter *William Aiken* was then tied up at the Southern Wharf on the Charleston waterfront and her commander, Captain Coste, was in a quandary. The *Aiken* flew the American ensign and the Revenue Marine Service pennant, and the Captain had taken the double oath of allegiance, both to the United States Government and the Revenue Marine Service. He attempted to get the cutter off the wharf but failed. Third Lieutenant Horace I. Gambrill, writing the journal for the day, does not say why the cutter was detained or why Captain Coste wanted to get her off. She remained at the wharf until December 26 when she "hauled off" and went around to her anchorage in the Ashley River off Chisholm's Rice Mill — today a Coast Guard station where there is still rice in the attic. Her American flag was still flying.

Second Lieutenant John A. Underwood wrote the events of December 27 in the journal. He said:

> Commences with fresh breezes from the NE and clear, middle part light variable airs, weather same, at 4 P.M. hauled down the Colors by order of Capt. Coste and discharged the crew, the vessel having been turned over by the Collector William F. Colcock, Esq. to the State of South Carolina.[2]

Beneath Underwood's entry Captain Coste wrote:

> Paid all the Officers and crew in full up to the 26th inst. inclusive on behalf of the U. States and discharged them.[3]

After several blank pages the journal was continued December 28 under the heading:

> Journal of the Schooner William Aiken
> N. L. Coste Captain, Service of the State of South Carolina.[4]

Under that date, Coste wrote:

> At 9 A.M. hoisted the Palmetto Flag and got underway and proceeded round to Cooper River at 10:30 A.M. anchored off Southern Wharf.[5]

He then went down the harbor to watch the movements of vessels and persons at Fort Sumter.

Why did the Captain take the cutter around to the Ashley River before he lowered the American flag? Did he have some last minute doubts about his course of action? He had been a loyal officer in the Revenue Marine Service since 1830, when he was commissioned a Second Lieutenant on the cutter *Marion* at Charleston. He was an expert navigator and pilot and had sailed cutters all along the coast from New London, Connecticut, to New Orleans. He piloted *Taney* and *Jackson* on inspection cruises and was commissioned Captain in 1842. During the War with Mexico, he was in command of the steam cutter *Legare* and was commended by the commodore of the cutter fleet, Captain John A. Webster, Sr. who said "Captain Coste deserves great credit for his exertions in filling up his coal, and perseverance in getting off." The *Legare* was a troublesome vessel, but in spite of a leaking and hazardous boiler, Coste sailed to Brazos Santiago, then to the mouth of the Rio Grande, and on to Vera Cruz and Anton Lizardo in 1846 on missions before going in to New Orleans for repairs.

After the war, he commanded *Crawford* and *Washington*. In 1853 he was commissioned to superintend the construction of *Caleb Cushing, James C. Dobbin, Robert McClelland,* and *James Campbell* at Somerset, Massachusetts. From 1854 to 1860, he commanded cutters in Charleston and Savannah.[6]

Some records say that his officers remained with him on board the *Aiken*[7], but all three—Lieutenants John Underwood, Henry O. Porter, and Horace J. Gambrill—left immediately for the North and were assigned to other cutters.[8]

On January 1, 1861, Captain Coste changed the name of the *Aiken's* journal. It was now called:

Journal of Revenue Cutter *Aiken*[9]

He reported seizing the United States Lighthouse Schooner *Howell Cobb*. Also
seized were two Coast Survey vessels, *Petrel* and *Firefly*. On January 10 he
changed the vessel's name again. Now he called the cutter a "Coast Police
Cutter." Her officers were listed as First Lieutenant Henry Mullings, Second
Lieutenant P. A. Auchile, Jr., and Third Lieutenant Napoleon E. Coste,
the Captain's son.[10]

With the Palmetto Flag flying on the *Aiken,* there were now only 23 cutters
in the Revenue Marine Service.

The *Dobbin* Escapes

A little further South, the cutter *James C. Dobbin* was in a perilous position.
Stationed at Savannah under command of Captain John A. Webster Jr., she
lay at anchor in the Savannah River unable to move. When word reached
Washington of the *Aiken's* seizure December 27, Captain Webster was ordered
to leave immediately for Baltimore, but the wind was from the East. Against
head winds he could not get down the narrow river to the sea, and Savannah's Customs Collector John Boston refused to furnish a tow.

East winds, "thick foggy weather", and "almost incessant rain" continued
all that week. There were at least two avowed Southerners, Third Lieutenant John G. Blackwood and First Lieutenant Alexander R. Abercrombie,
among the 17 men on board. Webster, a New Englander, was the son of Captain Webster, long a favorite in the Service. He was a Yankee, but he had
many friends in the South.

The *Dobbin* remained in Savannah over New Year's Day. On January 2,
Lieutenant Blackwood wrote in the journal:

No opportunity to get to sea, the Collector refusing to furnish a tow.[11]

The rain continued heavy the next night. About an hour after midnight,
there was a commotion outside and the cutter was boarded. Three officers —
Captain Webster, Second Lieutenant J. Fred Schultz, and Third Lieutenant
Blackwood signed the account in the Cutter's journal of the events that took
place January 3. They wrote:

Com'd heavy rain, and dense fog. About 1:30 A.M. the ship was sur-
rounded, boarded and taken forcible possession of by a large body of
armed men, who taking charge, secured the crew by placing them all
in irons and holding the officers as prisoners on parole. At daylight the
ship was got underway by the party in charge, and securing the services
of a passive tug, they towed down the River — setting the Palmetto Flag
at the peak and displaying the American ensign in the main rigging Union
down. At the top of high water, they run the vessel ashore on a spit in
the river and under the guns of the fort [Pulaski]. Taking all the boats
belonging to the vessel, they left for the Fort taking with them the ship's

crew. About 3 P.M., they returned on board accompanied by one of the Commanding Officers of the garrison at Fort Pulaski who assumed command of the cutter in the name of the State of Georgia, and strictly enjoined upon the Captain, Officers, and crew that any attempt to move the cutter would be considered hostile and would be treated accordingly by them. Ends clear with light westerly winds. Served 17 rations.[12]

Meantime, on shore, officials were astonished at the seizure. At the Custom House, Collector John Boston heard the news from Captain John Scriven early Friday morning, January 3. He immediately sent a message to Governor Joseph E. Brown at his home at Fort Pulaski. *Dobbin,* he said, had been seized by "parties unknown to me." He asked the Governor "the favor of you to direct those in charge to allow her to proceed to sea, in compliance with instructions from the office of the Secretary of the Treasury."[13]

The Governor immediately replied that he had ordered Colonel Lawton, commander at Fort Pulaski, "to protect Government property against injury." Boston was ordered to send a revenue boat to take the cutter into custody. The Governor's men would help haul her off the sand spit. She was to be allowed to proceed to sea at once.[14]

Brown wrote:

I much regret the lawless seizure of the vessel, and beg leave to assure you that I shall from time to time give such orders as will protect the Custom House and other property belonging to the Federal [government] till the action of this State is determined by the Convention of her people.[15]

All Friday morning the officers remained on the stranded cutter, pondering their future. About noon the steam tug *Samson* came down the river bringing the surveyor of the port and officers from Fort Pulaski. *Dobbin's* officers and crew were then released from custody. With the help of the *Samson,* the *Dobbin* was pulled off the sandspit. An officer and a boat were sent to the Fort for the cutter's belongings, and at 4 P.M., she was towed out to sea. Webster lost no time in crossing the bar and heading north.[16] Was he involved in the plot to seize the cutter? Northerners would wonder.

The *Dobbin* had had a narrow escape. There were still 23 cutters in the Revenue Marine Service.

The *Cass* Joins the South

At Mobile, Alabama, in January 1861, the cutter *Lewis Cass* was in poor condition. She was "leaking badly", and when underway, her pumps could not keep up with the water that came in. As a result, the vessel was out of trim with too much water in the bilge. The decks leaked too, soaking the bedding in the cabin and ward room.

Captain James J. Morrison appealed to the Mobile Customs Collector for repairs, but he would not listen. *Cass* continued to be sent out to board and examine vessels, sometimes as many as four or five a day.

On board in addition to Morrison were Lieutenants Anson S. Rogers, Charles G. Shoemaker and Thomas H. Lawrence, and nine in crew. The day after Christmas, the Captain went ashore to appeal again to the Collector for repairs, but none were promised. On New Year's Eve, the cutter was sent down the Bay to Red Bluff. Eleven days later, Alabama seceded from the Union, but it was not until January 30th when the cutter returned to Howard's wharf for water that she was seized by the State of Alabama.[17]

Captain Morrison resigned from the Revenue Marine Service the same day. He wrote Secretary of the Treasury John A. Dix saying:

> A Georgian by birth and an Alabaman by adoption, both States having assumed their independence — I desire to tender my resignation as a Captain of the Revenue Cutter Service to the Department.[18]

Morrison's name was stricken from the roles with the words "Tenders his resignation. Joins the South."[19]

Lieutenants Rogers, Lawrence, and Shoemaker wrote immediately asking for new assignments. Lawrence remarked that "pecuniary circumstances will oblige me to make this city my place of residence for the present. I hope this will meet the approbation of the department." Nevertheless, he and the other two men soon made their way North to new stations.[20] Rogers reported on the *Jackson* at Eastport, Maine, Lawrence on the *Cushing* at Portland, Maine, and Shoemaker on the *Campbell* at New London.[21]

There were now 22 cutters in the Revenue Marine Service.

Washington and *McClelland* Surrender

On October 24, 1860, there was a happy reunion off Slaughter House Point, New Orleans, when the 90-foot brig *Washington* rafted up to the somewhat smaller schooner cutter *Robert McClelland*. The *McClelland* had arrived ten days earlier from New York where she had been extensively repaired. It was now the *Washington's* turn to go to New York for repairs. The captains had been ordered to exchange officers and crews.

After inventories were taken, Captain Hudgins and his men transferred from the *McClelland* to the *Washington*. With him were his lieutenants, J. Wall Wilson, T. M. Dungan, and J. G. Hunt, and 13 in crew, including a young Scot named David Ritchie who was to witness and report dramatic events on the cutters late in January 1861. Lieutenant Anson S. Rogers took command of the *McClelland* with junior officer Samuel B. Caldwell and 11 in crew to assist him. The *McClelland* then "dropped off" and anchored nearby.[22]

Captain Hudgins was to have departed immediately for New York in the *Washington,* but he was still off Slaughter House Point November 27 when the order was countermanded and he was told to stay in New Orleans, and have the cutter repaired there. He sent his lieutenants North, dismissed his crew, and complained to the Treasury Department that he could not live ashore in New Orleans while the cutter was on the ways, for the $20 a month the government allowed.[23] Apparently, a more satisfactory arrangement was made, for he stayed in New Orleans and the *Washington* was laid up for repairs. Hudgins told the Secretary of the Treasury she would be ready for sea in April.

Meantime, the *McClelland* sailed down the Mississippi to cruise at the delta. In November her commander, Lieutenant Rogers, was sent to command the *Lewis Cass* at Mobile, and Captain John G. Breshwood of the *Cass* took command of the *McClelland*. Breshwood, a veteran of the service, was a native of Norfolk, Virginia, and well acquainted with many leaders in the South. He was described as a "representative of the Old Dominion and a warm hearted Republican." Although he had served on 11 cutters North and South and had fought in the War with Mexico in 1846, he had been dismissed from the service in 1849 when drastic cutbacks were made. After many protest by his friends, he was recommissioned in 1851. Among those who recommended him was John Slidell of Louisiana, later a prominent Confederate in the Civil War.[24]

During December, many vessels were boarded and examined, among them large passenger and cargo steamers from London, Liverpool, Greenock, Bristol, Glasgow, Rio di Janeiro, Boston, New York, and Havana. Most were reported to be in ballast, or carrying passengers, salt, coffee, and fruit. No slaves were mentioned in the *McClelland's* journal. A new officer, Lieutenant Thomas D. Fister, arrived in December. All three officers — Breshwood, Caldwell, and Fister — were avowed Southerners.[25]

Late in January, when the cutter was back in New Orleans, a special agent of the Treasury Department, J. H. Hemphill Jones, arrived in New Orleans to confer with the Customs Collector. He ordered Captain Breshwood to take the *McClelland* to New York.

According to a sworn statement made later by crew member David Ritchie, Jones appeared in the *McClelland's* cabin and ordered Breshwood to obey the order. Breshwood refused and was put in irons for disobedience. When Jones reported the situation to the Treasury Secretary, the Secretary wired back to put First Lieutenant Caldwell in command and "if anyone attempts to haul down the American flag, shoot him on the spot."[26] This was an idle gesture. Caldwell was as committed to the Confederacy as Breshwood. However, the American flag remained at the peak pro tem.

"About a week after this," Ritchie reported later, "the revenue flag was taken down from the *McClelland* and put in the signal house [a cupboard where flags are stored]. For about two weeks no flag was raised, then the secession flag was run up to the peak."[27]

On January 26, Louisiana seceded from the Union. On January 31 both *McClelland* and *Washington* were seized by the state. *McClelland* was taken into the Confederate Navy with Breshwood in command. The *Washington* was then on the ways. Her commander, Captain Hudgins, went North to report for duty.

Breshwood, Caldwell, and Fister all wrote formal notes of resignation to President Buchanan. Breshwood wrote:

> I have the honor to inform you that by Virtue of the Ordinance of the State of Louisiana my functions as Captain in the U.S. Rev. Service will cease and determine this day and I herewith tender my resignation."[28]

All three were stricken from the rolls of the Revenue Marine Service on February 18 by order of the President, Breshwood for having surrendered the *McClelland,* and Caldwell and Fister for having been parties to the surrender.[29]

There were now 20 cutters in the Revenue Marine Service.

The *Dodge* Tries to Hide

Although Texas seceded from the Union the first of February 1861, it was February 28 before Lieutenant William F. Rogers turned the cutter *Henry Dodge* over to the State. He tried to to keep her from being seized by hiding out in East Bay with a member of the United States Coast Survey on board.

Rogers was in command of the *Dodge* after her commander Captain Levy Harby was dismissed January 5. Revenue Marine records indicate that Harby had "joined the Confederacy." His dismissal seems to have been unknown to Secretary of the Treasury Howell Cobb for Cobb ordered him to Point Isabel soon after. Harby answered saying he was unwell and had left the cutter in charge of First Lieutenant Rogers.

The cutter was at the Government Wharf in Galveston Wednesday, January 30, when Rogers received orders dated January 22 from the Treasury Department to take her to New York. He knew she would never survive the voyage. Her bottom was so foul and worm-eaten that she did not respond to the tiller but constantly fell off course. Only minor repairs had been made since she was severely damaged in a gale while on an official cruise to Vera Cruz, Mexico the previous March. However, if she remained in Galveston, she was in danger of being seized by the mobs on the waterfront.

For two days Lieutenant Rogers tried to decide what to do. He talked to Lieutenant Stevens of the Lighthouse Department and to his friend, Lieutenant Bell of the United States Coast Survey. Bell, who had been sent South to survey East Bay at Galveston, suggested that they take the cutter to the Bay. A decision was made on Saturday when Lieutenant William G. Roche wrote in the journal:

> After a confidential consultation, a report of her unseaworthiness, and the excited state of the public mind on shore and the threats to take the Vessel, he [Rogers] deemed it most prudent upon application of Lieut. Bell U.S.A. to take the Vessel up East Bay to assist him in his Surveys.[30]

Lieutenant Bell came on board Monday. They sailed in the afternoon and spent the night alongside the wharf at Pelican Spit discharging ballast so they could get over the reef at the bay entrance. There were 10 men on board. On Wednesday, they warped the *Dodge* over the reef, stood up the Bolivar Channel, and came to anchor north northeast of Ladies Pass. The following day Rogers sent a boat to Galveston for mail and news. On Friday Lieutenant Bell took the cutter's other boat, and with Lieutenant Roche and several members of the crew, left to survey the eastern part of the bay.

The surveying party was absent until Saturday, February 16. On the 18th, Rogers sent a boat to town for mail and news and on the 22nd, he himself left the cutter and went into Galveston to see what was happening. The water-front was in an uproar. Rogers felt there was no use holding out, especially with rations and water getting low on the cutter. Returning to East Bay, he prepared the *Dodge* for a return to the city. She sailed, against a head wind, February 25th, and was so sluggish that the captain was forced to anchor the next night two miles below the city. It was February 27th before she reached Galveston. "For reasons before mentioned," as the Journal reports, "she came to anchor not off the Government Wharf but off the 'upper wharves.'"

The next day, Mr. Butler from the Custom House came on board and paid off the officers and crew for the month of February. He reported that the Collector of the Customs refused to sign any requisitions for the month of March.

On March 2, the *Dodge* was turned over to the Quartermaster of the Confederate States of America at Houston, Texas.[31] Lieutenant Tennison had left several days before on a month's leave of absence to see his family in Washington. He had tendered his resignation before leaving, but on February 28, he wrote the Secretary of the Treasury that this was "in the heat of the moment" and he regretted it. It was not, he said, "from any feeling for either the North or the South." Tennison was allowed to remain in the service. He was ordered to the *Varina* at New York but was dismissed later in 1861 for intoxication.

Lieutenants Rogers and Roche both resigned on March 2 to join the Confederacy. Ironically, Rogers was commissioned a Captain in the Revenue Marine Service on March 1.[32]

There were now 19 cutters in the Revenue Marine Service.

The *Duane* is Attacked

In Norfolk, Virginia, although the waterfront seethed with talk of secession, the cutter *William J. Duane* continued her usual duties of boarding and examining the vessels that passed in Chesapeake Bay, and of visiting the lightships. Then abruptly, on February 17, she was ordered by the Treasury Secretary to "get ready for sea" and sail to New York.

The next few days were spent in feverish activity. The *Duane* received many supplies, including "blocks" of matches, a 28-second glass, candles, a log line, and a dozen sail needles.

She was commanded by Captain Richard Evans who made haste to obey orders. As the journal for February 18 reports:

> Crew employed through the day overhauling and refitting fore and jib sheet block straps, making chafing gear for the rigging, marking deep sea lead line and getting ready for sea.[33]

Then the order was revoked. On February 20, a telegram was received from the Secretary ordering Captain Evans to await further instruction.

The next day the *James C. Dobbin* arrived and anchored close to the *Duane*. After her narrow escape from being seized by Secessionists at Savannah, she put in for repairs. She did not stay long, no doubt fearing another seizure. On March 1, Captain Evans was relieved of the command of the *Duane*. His place was taken by Captain Hudgins, a Southerner but not then a Secessionist, who was ordered to dismiss the crew, place the lieutenants on temporary leave, and superintend extensive repairs on the cutter.[34] Hudgins was so short-handed he took the responsibility of employing a man and two boys to guard the vessel. The cutter was threatened by angry mobs along the waterfront while under repair in March and April.

Lieutenant James G. Milligan, one of the men on leave, asked to be retained as a Lieutenant, and when his request was denied, wrote the following letter to the new Secretary of the Treasury, Salmon P. Chase, April 15:

As I believe the principles coercion to be submersive to the institution of the United States spirit as it would be incompatible with my moral convictions of thought to sustain a Rights as enunciated and set forth by the immortal Jefferson and Madison in the Virginia and Kentucky Resolutions of 98,99, *I hereby most respectfully resign my position as a First Lieutenant in the United States Revenue Service.* In doing so I have within me a peace above all [unintelligible] dignities a still and quiet conscience, consoled with the assurance that I have ever and at all times done my Duty to the best of my ability and never under any circumstances have I betrayed any Federal trust reposed in me by the Constitution (obligations required of me upon sworn in to office.)"[35]

Two days later Virginia seceded from the Union. *Duane's* guns were then seized by an angry mob. As Captain Hudgins wrote to Secretary Chase April 18:

I have to report to the Dept. that about 3 o'clock yesterday a large party of men and boys headed by R. B. Ball, Alex Santos, Edward L. Young and McCoant, citizens of Norfolk, came to the old Customs House, and took possession of the three guns, one 18 and two 32 pr., shot, ballast and water tanks belonging to the Revenue Cutter "Duane" and removed them to the City Hall. I asked one of the parties, R. B. Ball, by what authority he and his party were seizing and removing the public property. He replied that they were acting under the order of the Mayor of the city. I called on that functionary this morning to ascertain the facts in the case and he assured me that he knew nothing whatever of the transaction until some time after it had happened, and learning early last night that an attempt would be made to force the doors of the old Custom House for the purpose of removing the two 32 Pr. guns and other public property stored there, he detailed a police force to guard the premises during the night with instructions to see no one entered the building. He very emphatically disavowed the act of the Mob, and assured me that he would today write Governor Letcher informing him of the circumstances and request him to have the public property seized by the Mob returned to the place where it was taken from and also that a strong Military guard be placed over it to protect it from further molestation.[36]

The Federal shipyard was in a state of turmoil, Navy officers having delayed too long in removing the government vessels. Only the warship *Cumberland* got away. Seven vessels were burnt April 20, but the Navy warship *Merrimack* and the Revenue Cutter *Dodge* escaped total destruction. The Southerners had other plans for them.

Captain Hudgins resigned and joined the Confederacy the day the Navy Yard was seized, saying he owed allegiance to "none other than my native state, Virginia." His younger brother, William, also in the Revenue Marine, resigned the same day.[37]

There were now only 18 vessels in the Revenue Marine Service.

Millard Fillmore

PRESIDENT OF THE UNITED STATES OF AMERICA,

To all who shall see these presents, Greeting:

Know ye, *That reposing special trust and confidence in the integrity, diligence, and good conduct of John M. Gowan I do appoint him Captain of a Cutter in the service of the* United States, *for the protection of the revenue; and do authorize and empower him to execute and fulfil the duties of that office according to law: And to have and to hold the said office, with all the rights and privileges thereunto legally appertaining unto him the said John M. Gowan during the pleasure of the President of the* United States for the time being.

IN TESTIMONY WHEREOF, *I have caused these letters to be made patent, and the seal of the Treasury Department of the* United States *to be hereunto affixed.*

GIVEN *under my hand, at the City of Washington, the third day of December in the year of our Lord one thousand eight hundred and fifty two and of the Independence of the United States of America the Seventy Seventh*

By the President: *Millard Fillmore*

Tho Corwin ✳ **Secretary of the Treasury.**

Commission of Captain John McGowan

CHAPTER IV

The First Shot

Late in the war, President Lincoln told his friend Isaac Schemerhorn of New York that the Civil War had been initiated by the Confederates when they fired on *Star of the West.*[1] By that time both sides were trying to disclaim responsibility for starting the dreadful conflict.

Star of the West was a merchant vessel owned by M. O. Roberts of Brooklyn. She was a paddle-wheel steamer, built in New York in 1852 and registered for transatlantic trade in 1860. She was used on the run from New York to Aspinwall on the Isthmus of Panama.[2]

Soon after South Carolina seceded from the Union and seized all government property, except Fort Sumter, Roberts was secretly approached by President Buchanan's agents. Would he charter the steamer for an expedition to Charleston to reinforce and supply the troops under Major Anderson who were holding the fort?

Some men in Washington, including Gustavus Fox, wanted to send an armed fleet against the recalcitrant city but others objected, hoping for a peaceful settlement. *Star of the West* was to go unarmed except for one brass cannon.

Roberts agreed to the charter, asking $1500 a day, and coal. He settled for $1500 without coal, and by January 5, had the vessel ready for sea.[3]

Ex-Revenue Marine Officer McGowan in Command

At the helm of the *Star of the West* was Captain John McGowan, formerly a lieutenant in the Revenue Marine Service. He had served 16 years as an officer before he was obliged to resign in 1853 in order to support his "numerous family".[4] He had been commissioned a Third Lieutenant on the *Campbell* at Baltimore in 1837 and had served on *Woodbury, Forward,* and *Bibb*

Steamship *Star of the West*

Harper's Weekly

before being dispatched on *Bibb* during the War with Mexico in 1846. He was one of a group of Revenue Marine men who went ashore at Tabasco and captured the town.

In 1847-49 at Baltimore, he was ordered to superintend the building of *William J. Duane* and *Crawford* at Philadelphia. In 1852 he was commissioned Captain, after taking the cutter *Polk* to the Pacific. Captain William W. Polk recommended him, saying "I know you, Sir, to be a sailor, and officer and a gentleman."[5] Captain Henry B. Nones commended him for his actions at Alvarez and Tabasco in the War with Mexico. Captain Henry D. Hunter called him "one of the best navigators in the Service."[6] In 1849 Treasury Secretary Meredith congratulated him for "efficient aid rendered the Packet Ship *Tusacrora* near Cape Henlopen."[7] His resignation in 1853 was accepted with regret, but none coulld deny that his "numerous family" would be better supported by the pay in the merchant marine.[8]

As master of merchant vessels he continued to be highly respected. When in command of *Empire City,* he was given a $1,000 reward for recovering "treasure" (money) and valuable cargo from the steamship *Illinois* wrecked on coral rocks on the coast of Cuba. His "skill, ability, and seamanship" were highly praised.[9]

He had commanded *Star of the West* for some time. To avoid suspicion, the steamer was secretly laden with supplies at her pier at the foot of Warren Street, New York, and cleared for New Orleans and Savannah. At sunset on January 5, 1861, she left the pier and steamed down to Governor's Island. Here, in darkness, she took on four Army officers, 250 artillery men and marines with their arms and ammunitions.[10]

The *Star* Departs

She passed Sandy Hook at nine o'clock that night and headed South. Meantime word had reached Washington from Major Anderson at Charleston that he was willing to hold out with what troops he had until his supplies were exhausted, and that any unarmed vessel would be destroyed by the strong batteries at the harbor's entrance if it attempted to reach him. All buoys had been removed from the approaches to the harbor, and all lights in the city were doused at night. A telegram was sent from Washington to stop the *Star of the West.* It arrived after she had sailed. There was no way to reach her.

McGowan sailed on, not knowing that Anderson had warned him away and that spies in Washington had already informed Charleston that he was en route. He approached the coast of South Carolina, and early on the morning of January 9, reached Charleston bar at half past one. The *Star of the West* was anchored until dawn with lights extinguished. At dawn she was spotted by the scouting Confederate steamer *General Clinch* who immediately sent up flares and spread the alarm. McGowan got underway, ordered all troops below, and approached the harbor. He was within two miles of the Fort when a shot ricocheted across his bow from a hidden battery on Morris Island marked by a Palmetto Flag.[11]

The *Star of the West* carried the American flag at her peak, but as she neared the Fort, McGowan unfurled another American flag 40 feet long and had it hoisted at the bow to attract the attention of Anderson. The garrison at the Fort watched with delight as the flag unfolded. They had not, until then, identified the vessel as any but another commercial steamer.

More shots were now fired from Morris Island on the port side. Then came two shots from rebels at Fort Moultrie on the starboard side. McGowan's one small brass gun remained silent.

At Fort Sumter guns were shotted, run out, and brought to bear on Fort Moutrie and the positions on Morris Island. Major Anderson hesitated to fire since Fort Sumter itself had not been attacked, and he was not aware of the *Star of the West's* official assignment.

Shot after shot was aimed at the vessel as she neared Sumter, some falling short, some bounding over her deck and through her rigging. One struck her in the fore-chains and one was later reported by Captain McGowan to have come "within an ace of carrying away our rudder." Still, he waited for some response from Major Anderson. Meantime two steam tugs put out from the city of Charleston, one of them towing an armed schooner. This may have been the former Revenue Cutter *William Aiken* which surrendered to South Carolina on December 27, 1860. McGowan faced the loss of his vessel and the priceless human cargo below decks if he proceeded. After 17 shots had been fired at him, he prudently spun his wheel around and headed for the open sea. He was back at the Warren Street pier in New York April 12 with the *Star of the West* intact and all the soldiers and his own crew alive and well. [12]

Captain Mcgowan was severely criticized for failing to reach Major Anderson. Later in the war, he wrote that he had "suffered severely in reputation for this affair, being condemned by Mr. Roberts because I brought the command away safe instead of sinking a steamer of doubtful reputation." [13] He was then back in the service and asking to be sent "where there is some hard service to be done." [14]

McGowan continued in the service of M. O. Roberts until August 13, 1861, when he was re-commissioned a captain in the Revenue Marine Service. [15]

The months of January through April 1861 were dark and hectic for the Union. The Revenue Marine Service drifted along under the supervision of Philip Francis Thomas, who was appointed Secretary of the Treasury when Howell Cobb left to join the Confederacy in January. John A. Dix took Thomas's place in mid-January. Some of the cutter officers had no idea who was Secretary of the Treasury. They sent their letters to "Hon. Secretary of the Treasury." Dix remained in office until Lincoln was inaugurated (March 4) when Samuel Portland Chase was appointed to head the Department.

The *Lucky Dobbin* and the *Forward*

Two of the cutters, *Dobbin* and *Forward,* narrowly escaped being seized, *Dobbin* not once but three times. After her miraculous escape in Savannah and an equally miraculous escape from a gale off Hatteras on her way North, she reached Baltimore much in need of repairs. During the gale she had "doubled" Cape Hatteras and then had been thrown back twice into the Gulf Stream. Nearing Norfolk she had been driven on the False Cape, where she had anchored to keep from going ashore, and then had to "slip moorings" and leave a valuable anchor in the sea to gain an offing.[16]

After repairs at Baltimore, Captain Webster was ordered back to Norfolk to cruise at the entrance to Chesapeake Bay, where the climate was then decidedly unhealthy for Union vessels. He did not protest the assignment but deplored the fact that he had but two officers on board, Lieutenants Edgar Murden and Fred Schultz. On February 21, he arrived at Norfolk, and wrote Secretary Dix:

"I have the Honor to inform the Department that I have arrived with the Rev. Cutter James C. Dobbin at Norfolk, Va. and reported according to instructions to the Collector of that Port."[17]

There were some in Washington who questioned Webster's loyalty, as they questioned the loyalty of many of the officers who had served in Southern stations and had friends in the South, but he remained loyal. Once more, in April at Norfolk, he narrowly escaped having his cutter seized. He was still stationed there after Virginia had seceded from the Union April 15, and angry mobs had attacked the cutter *Duane* April 17. That same night Webster received word that the *Dobbin* would also be attacked. He wasted no time in getting away and going up the coast to Wilmington, Delaware.[18] He wrote the new Secretary of the Treasury Chase April 21 from Wilmington, saying:

"Having received information from a reliable source at Fortress Monroe on the evening of the 17th inst. that obstructions had been placed in the channel of the Elizabeth River (at Norfolk), that the Virginia Convention had passed the Secession Act, and that a strong expedition was fitting out to attack this vessel, I deemed it my duty, being unable any longer to enforce the Revenue Laws in the waters of Virginia, for the safety of the vessel to repair to this place, where I have this day arrived and await further orders."[19]

He soon found that Wilmington was no safer than Norfolk. Captain Henry B. Nones,[20] stationed there on the cutter *Forward,* was also apprehensive. On April 20, Webster wrote the Secretary that there were "respectable" citizens in Wilmington backing plans to secede from the Union and seize the public property, including the cutters.[21]

Upon receipt of Webster's letter from Norfolk, Secretary Chase sent a letter to Wilmington ordering him to Philadelphia. The Wilmington Collector countermanded the order and told him to cruise in Delaware Bay. Chase then instructed Captain Webster to proceed *immediately* to Philadelphia. He arrived at the Philadelphia Navy Yard May 1, having lost two officers, Lieutenants Blackwood and Alex R. Abercrombie, to the Confederacy while at Wilmington.[22]

The *Dobbin* had escaped from the Secessionists three times. She was to serve throughout the Civil War and to continue her charmed life until 1881, serving as the first "practice" or "school" ship from 1877 to her sale at New Bedford, Massachusetts, for $5,166 on April 6, 1881.[23]

The *Forward* also left Wilmington for Philadelphia. Captain Nones wrote Chase April 25 saying:

> I have the honor to report to the department the inefficient condition of the U.S. Cutter Forward under my command. Her Battery as well as her small arms are almost useless, and in her present conditions badly calculated for a defence. I am of the opinion that an attempt may be made to get possession of the Cutter. Indeed I am convinced that a plot now exists, headed by respectable persons, to make an attempt to capture her. I have, in view of the condition of things, run her up the river for her safety.[24]

In addition to having six cutters seized by the rebels between December 1860 and April 1861, the Treasury Department received a stream of resignations from officers, some of them with long and honorable records. They included Captains Napoleon L. Coste, Levy C. Harby, Richard Evans, William B. Whitehead, Osmond Peters, James J. Morrison, John G. Breshwood, Robert K. Hudgins, and Lieutenants Edgar O. Murden, William E. Hudgins, James F. Milligan, Samuel B. Caldwell, Thurston M. Taylor, John R. C. Lewis, John G. Blackwood, John J. Hunt, Bushrod W. Frobel, Johnston de Lagnelle, Marshall Brown, Thomas Fister, William G. Roche, Thomas Moffett, Alexander Abercrombre and William F. Rogers.

The Distant Cutters

The commencement of hostilities had little effect on the six cutters on the Great Lakes. By December all of them were in winter quarters waiting for Spring to thaw the ice in the lakes. On the West Coast the *William L. Marcy*, in California, the *Joseph Lane* in Oregon Territory and the *Jefferson Davis* in Washington Territory continued their normal operations, slow to learn that Confederate vessels were on the prowl for Union ships laden with gold dust.

There were many Southern sympathizers along the Pacific, and it was ironic that two of the cutters — the *Joseph Lane* and the *Jefferson Davis* — were named for Secessionists, one for Governor Lane of Oregon who had dropped out of public life and retreated to his home in Oregon, and the other for the man who became President of the Confederates States of America.

Chief Engineer William C. Davis of the Navy, among others, was upset by these names. He wrote Secretary Chase saying:

> Union loving people on this coast would be much pleased to have the foregoing names deleted and names better suited to the times substituted.[25]

The names were never changed. Nor were the names of the six Great Lakes cutters, all of them honoring public officers who defected to the South.

CHAPTER V

The Navy and the Revenue Marine

Fort Sumter remained the major issue when Lincoln took office March 4. One of his first actions was to consult his chief aides on provisioning the men who held the Fort against great odds. On March 15, he wrote:

> Assuming it to be possible to now provision Fort Sumter under all the circumstances is it wise to attempt it?[1]

Of those consulted only Secretary Chase felt this could be accomplished without provoking a war. Secretary of State Seward said he "would not provoke war in any way now" and Secretary of the Navy Gideon Welles wrote "I do not think it wise." Even the officers at the Fort argued against it.[2]

While the debate continued, Lincoln began counting his resources. He wrote Chase asking how many vessels would be needed off shore, in addition to the revenue cutters, to protect the revenue. Chase replied that he had no vessels off shore south of North Carolina, and that all 11 revenue cutters in patrol service would have to be rearmed. At least three of them, he said, would have to be replaced by steamships and three storage ships would be required.[3]

Lincoln then communicated with the Secretary of the Navy, saying:

> Sir: I shall be obliged if you will inform me what amount of naval force you could at once place at the control of the revenue service, and also whether at some distance of time you could so place an additional force, and how much and at what time?[4]

Welles replied March 20 saying that he would put 12 Navy vessels under control of the Revenue Service but "the amount in the future would depend on the number of men allowed the Navy." He also thought that four vessels could be withdrawn from foreign service within eight months, and that seven of the Navy vessels not in commission could be made available for the West Coast.[5]

There is no record in Coast Guard history of Navy vessels being turned over to the Revenue Marine. Meantime Lincoln had ordered the transfer of the *Harriet Lane* from the Revenue Marine to the Navy, on a temporary basis, with her Revenue Marine personnel, including Captain John Faunce, on board. The cutter was then stationed at the Battery in New York Harbor where she seized vessels suspected of slave trading. She now had 71 men in her crew, all of them, by January 10, 1861, being drilled at arms. Some, "small arms men," were called "infantry." Others, including the crews of her launches, were known as "rifle men." Drills were frequent, starting in January. In February the cutter was overhauled at the Brooklyn Navy Yard, and "all her standing rigging, fore and aft [was] greased with pork rind."[6]

On March 6, *Harriet Lane* seized the brig *Cora*, suspected of slaving, and turned her over to the Surveyor of the Port. She continued to board a dozen or more vessels a day until she was ordered into the Navy. The last vessel boarded before she went into the Navy was the *John Oliver* of Edgartown, bringing rice from Charleston to New York.[7]

In spite of the fact that there was still disagreement about the wisdom of sending an expedition to Fort Sumter, Navy Secretary Gideon Welles ordered a "peaceable" mission to proceed under the direction of Gustavus V. Fox. His fleet was to include the small Navy vessels *Pocohontas* and *Pawnee*, the chartered *Baltic*, the revenue cutter *Harriet Lane*, and the powerful *Powhatan*, commanded by Captain Samuel Mercer. The Navy was to supply the fleet with one month's stores and 300 men, the Army with 200 artillery men, 12 month's supplies, three tugs and a large steamer.[8]

Lincoln approved the plan and on April 5, Navy Secretary Welles sent the following letter to Captain John Faunce "Commander of Steamer Harriet Lane":

> "Sir: The Harriet Lane under your command having been detached from the collection district of New York, and assigned to duty under the Navy Department, you are hereby instructed to proceed to within ten miles due east from and off Charleston light house, where you will report to Captain Mercer, of the Powhatan, for duty, on the morning of the 11th instant; and should he not be there, you will wait a reasonable time for his arrival."[9]

A Boisterous Passage

Faunce wasted no time in obeying orders. He sailed from New York at nine o'clock in the morning April 8, and was the first of the fleet to reach the designated spot. He reported his arrival to Gideon Welles in a message dated April 11, saying:

> I have the honor to report the arrival of the above mentioned vessel at this port ten miles from Charleston bar after a boisterous passage of 75 miles.[10]

Baltic, with Fox on board, and *Pocahontas* were the next to arrive. While they waited at the bar for the *Powhatan* (the big warship that was to lead the fleet into the harbor) and three tugs, Major Anderson was facing a crisis in Fort Sumter. He had promised the Confederates that he would evacuate the Fort if no provisions had arrived by April 15, but at 3:20 A.M. April 12, he was notified by Confederate General Beauregard that Southern forces would open fire on the fort in one hour.

At six o'clock in the morning on April 12, the firing began. At almost the same time the *Pawnee* arrived at the rendez-vous. The *Powhatan* was still missing. Fox was left with two small Navy vessels, the chartered *Baltic* and the Revenue Cutter *Harriet Lane*. The three tugs never appeared. One had not left New York; one had been driven by the storm into Wilmington, Delaware, and one had gone to Savannah. *Powhatan* had by-passed Charleston and gone on to Pensacola, Florida, by order of President Lincoln.[11]

In a major mix-up, President Lincoln had ordered the *Powhatan* to Pensacola and changed her command without notifying Secretary of the Navy Welles. Shortly before she was scheduled to leave New York for Charleston, Captain David Dixon Porter had arrived on board off Staten Island and handed Captain Mercer orders that countermanded those of Secretary Welles. Mercer went ashore and the *Powhatan*, with Porter at the helm, left for Pensacola. In fact, Lincoln had deliberately deceived Welles and Fox when he relieved Captain Mercer from the command of *Powhatan*, replacing him with Captain David Dixon Porter, and ordered the powerful war vessel to by-pass Charleston and proceed to Fort Pickens at Pensacola, Florida. While she was still at the Brooklyn Navy Yard, he had written the yard's Commander Foote saying:

> She is bound on Secret service and you will under no circumstances communicate to the Navy Department the fact that she is fitting out.[12]

Not knowing what had happened to the *Powhatan,* Fox tried to lead his decimated fleet into Charleston harbor. The *Pocahontas* chose to remain behind while the other three ventured nearer the Fort. The *Baltic* led the way, followed by *Harriet Lane* and *Pawnee*. By then, firing at the Fort was already intense. The vessels were in danger of being caught in cross fire between Sumter and Moultrie as well as fire from Morris Island. Fox gave the signal to retreat. *Harriet Lane* and *Baltic* turned away. The *Pawnee* continued on for a short distance and then joined them. All three were soon out of range of the big guns of both nations.[13]

That morning, the *Harriet Lane* met an oncoming steamer flying no flag, and true to her Revenue Marine Service traditions, ordered the vessel to come to and show her colors. The vessel ignored the signals and the *Harriet Lane* fired across her bow, whereupon the vessel falsely hoisted an American flag and was allowed to proceed. The vessel was actually the Confederate steamer *Nashville* and in firing on her, the *Harriet Lane* is said to have fired the first shot of the Civil War from a vessel. The shot was fired by Lieutenant Daniel D. Thompkins.

"I Know But Little About Ships"

After the fiasco at Charleston, Lincoln apologized to Fox in a letter May 1.[15] The failure of the expedition, he said, was due in part to the tugs being detained by a gale, and to the absence of *Powhatan*. He said:

> By an accident for which you were in no way responsible, and possibly I to some extent was, you were deprived of a war vessel with her men which you deemed of great importance to the enterprise.[16]

Lincoln, the midwesterner, admitted that he had little knowledge of ships and shipping, but he was quick to establish the Atlantic blockade April 19 which led eventually to the defeat of the rebels. From his vantage point at the White House he could see the Potomac and Anacostia Rivers, and apparently kept a close watch on the vessels that came and went at the Washington Navy Yard. On April 23, he wrote Welles saying:

> I think I see three vessels go up to the Navy Yard just now. Will you please send down and learn what they are?[17]

He took an interest in mariners too, although he did not speak or spell their language. On May 14, he wrote Welles saying:

> I know but little about ships, but I feel a good deal of interest for George W. Lawrence of Maine, who is proficient in that line. I believe it is settled that the Gov't. has large use for the barches [sic] of Maine and I shall be glad if Mr. Lawrence can be engaged in it on fair terms to himself and to us.[18]

The "barches" were used to transport troops.

Abraham Lincoln

PRESIDENT OF THE UNITED STATES OF AMERICA,

To all who shall see these presents, Greeting:

Know ye, That reposing special trust and confidence in the integrity, diligence, and good conduct of *William A. Howard* I do appoint him *Captain* to take rank fr 3 in the Register, of a Cutter in the service of the United States, for the protection of the revenue; and do authorize and empower him to execute and fulfil the duties of that office according to law: And to have and to hold the said office, with all the rights and privileges thereunto legally appertaining, unto him, the said *William A. Howard* during the pleasure of the President of the United States for the time being.

IN TESTIMONY WHEREOF, I have caused these letters to be made patent, and the seal of the Treasury Department of the United States to be hereunto affixed.

GIVEN under my hand, at the City of Washington, the *twentieth* day of *April* in the year of our Lord one thousand eight hundred and *Sixty one* and of the Independence of the United States of America the *Eighty fifth*. —

By the President: *Abraham Lincoln*

Salmon P. Chase Secretary of the Treasury.

Commission of Captain William A. Howard
National Archives

CHAPTER VI

The Rise and Fall of Captain Howard

On April 20, Captain William A. Howard was called back to the United States Revenue Marine Service "to take general charge of arming and equipping and assigning to stations the revenue vessels." He was to assist Secretary Chase, Chase's assistant, George R. Harrington, and the New York Customs Collector Hiram Barney.[1]

The Captain had been a noted figure in the development of the Revenue Marine Service from 1831, when he was commissioned to command the tiny cutter *Swiftsure* at Eastport, Maine, to 1849 when the service was reduced and he was dismissed. He was not in the good graces of Superintendent Alexander V. Fraser. From Eastport he had gone to New York and then Norfolk. In 1833 he was referred to as a "superintendent" and is said to have supervised the equipment of the five cutters that were sent to Charleston during the nullification difficulties. He took a year's furlough in 1835 returning to command the *McLane* at New Bedford and later at New Orleans. He then served for a year on the *Madison* at Portsmouth, New Hampshire. In 1838 he resigned, but four years later, he was recommissioned Captain to prepare models for two iron steam cutters, *Legare* and *Bibb*, each about 160 feet long and costing about $90,000. The *Legare*, the first steam cutter, was sent to Norfolk; the *Bibb* was sent to New Orleans with Captain Howard in command.

In 1846-1847, Captain Howard played a major role in the Mexican-American War, as commander of the revenue steamer *McLane*. He aided Commodore Perry U.S.N. in the attack on Frontera, Tabasco and Alvarado and helped to capture 11 vessels from Yucatan which had been supplying the enemy with munitions. He also assisted the Army. He was one of three revenue cutter officers commended for gallantry in action.

The steam cutters were not a success, and those connected with their construction fell out of political favor. Congress ordered the number of officers greatly reduced. Howard was dismissed, but in the meantime, he had superintended the transformation of the steam cutter *Polk* into a sailing bark.[2]

From 1849 to 1861, he remained in the shipping business in New York. Called back to public duty by Secretary Chase when war began, he was recommissioned Captain and ranked Number 3 on the Revenue Marine Register. The two highest ranking officers were Captains John A. Webster, Sr. and Henry D. Hunter.

On April 29, Howard was told by Chase that he had ordered *Jackson* and *Campbell* to New York, *Cushing* to Boston, and *Forward* and *Dobbin* to Philadelphia, withdrawing all five from revenue duties. They were to be armed by Howard for "any service that the exigencies of the Treasury Department might demand of them," including participation in the Atlantic Blockade then being organized. To replace them in their regular revenue work, he directed Howard to examine the Coast Survey vessels and select those that were acceptable. Howard was now classified in the Treasury Department as being on "special duty" and was given permission to purchase arms from the Navy for the cutters. He called himself a "senior captain."[3]

The same day, Howard wrote "Friend Harrington" (Assistant Secretary of the Treasury Harrington) asking for a list of officers on leave, and of officers of vessels in the Coast Survey. On May 31, the steam cutters *Bibb* and *Corwin* and the sailing cutters *Arago, Varina, Vixen,* and *Crawford* were transferred from the Coast Survey to the Revenue Marine. The *Bibb* was stationed at Kill Von Kull, Staten Island, the *Varina* at New Bedford, the *Crawford* at New York, the *Corwin* at Baltimore, and the *Arago* at New York. The *Arago* was used as a troop ship, shuttling government personnel between New York and Hilton Head, and the others as guard ships and also for transporting troops and other duties that did not take them out to sea.[4]

Howard then made a list of all the cutters and officers, the condition of the cutters, and the loyalty of the officers. Some suspicion attached to young Captain Webster in connection with the *Dobbin's* capture at Savannah. Captain Faunce was asked to investigate. Lieutenant Tennison of the seized cutter *Dodge* at Mobile had appeared in New York looking for a future assignment but had "disgraced the service by drunkeness — rolling around the streets." Howard asked that he be dismissed.[5]

In a letter to Secretary Chase, May 2, he asked for ten copies each of the Telegraphic Dictionary, the Signal Book, and Lockwoods Manual for Midshipmen. He was then completing work on transforming *Varina* and *Crawford* into armed Revenue Cutters, calling them "two fine schooners." They remained in the Service throughout the war. The others, *Bibb, Arago, Corwin,* and *Vixen* were back in the Coast Survey before the end of 1861, having served their purpose for what Howard called "temporary deficiencies" in the Service.

After visiting Philadelphia in May, he wrote Secretary Chase that the *Philip Allen* was "totally unworthy of repairs" but could be used as a guard ship in New York Harbor. He would transfer her officers to either *Crawford* or *Varina* and man her with an inspector and boat's crew for boarding purposes. This he felt, would stop the New Yorkers who persisted in sending arms and ammunition to the rebels. In this Howard did not get his wish. The *Philip Allen* remained on duty in Chesapeake Bay throughout the war.[6]

Captain Howard Reports

In mid-May, Howard went to Washington for a week to consult with Secretary Chase and Assistant Secretary Harrington. While there he wrote a number of letters to Chase, among them one written May 18 describing the cutters on the Atlantic Coast. He wrote:

I have the honor to report: The Revenue Cutter Service on the Atlantic Coast consists of seven schooners and one side wheel steamer [The *Harriet Lane* was still considered to be in the Revenue Marine Service.], the former ranging from 110 to 140 tons each. They are allowed by Law, One Captain and Three Lieutenants with Seventy Seamen, Petty Officers, & boys included. For several years past they have had so few men, that to work the vessel, get her underway with a boats crew away was impossible, also to man a Prize. The size of the present vessels (Harriet Lane always excepted) will not permit the berthing of the prescribed crew. The Cutters were so badly armed that the commonest armed Vessel would be more than a match for them. Recently however by order of the Department one long 32-pounder rifled Gun has been placed on board Each Cutter viz "Morris", "C Cushing", "Campbell", & "Dobbin" with a crew of Forty men. The "Jackson" belonging to the Eastport station had not arrived on Friday last but hourly expected when (if worthy of it) she will be armed & manned in similar manner.

The Steamers, "Corwin", "Bibb", & "Vixen" (C.S.) are cruising in the harbor of New York. The "Vixen" is incapable of mounting an armament for sea service, but can be made available for harbor duties. The "Bibb" with some considerable expense can be made a serviceable cruising vessel with a respectable armament. The steamer "Corwin" is the best vessel, has now mounted two 12 pounder medium Guns (mounted by me) and is capable of carrying a still heavier Battery, and would be an effective vessel. The "Philip Allen" is unworthy of repairs. The "Forward" is at present co-operating with the Army at Annapolis. She mounts 1 Long 18 pounder and 4-12 pounder guns. She is reported to be in bad condition, but this statement must be erroneous as she has been thoroughly repaired within one year.

The "Joseph Lane" is on her way from the Pacific Coast, daily expected. I am unacquainted with her present condition and capacity. [*Joseph Lane* remained in the Pacific.]

The Schs "Crawford" and "Varina" (taken from C. Survey) have been strengthened and armed. Each with a rifled 32 pounder Gun amidships, they will be efficient vessels as permanent Cutters.

There are Eight or Ten smaller vessels belonging to the Coast Survey, that will answer for temporary duty as Revenue Cutters, but entirely too small for permanent Cutters.

Officers — consists of Nineteen (19) Captains, Fourteen (14) First Lieutenants, Fifteen (15) Second Lieutenants, Nineteen (19) Third

Lieutenants. Six of the Captains are in my opinion unfitted by age, sickness, and otherwise for service — however ungrateful the task may be, I must from a sense of duty name them, if called upon by the Hon. Secretary of the Treasury so to do. Such is also the case of several of the First Lieutenants but inasmuch as the want of professional knowledge will be discovered by an Examining Board I consider it unnecessary to designate them — even if I had not been absent from service several years.

The want of Esprit du Corps I do not consider entirely the fault of the Officers themselves. The curtailment of crews and of everything that gave efficiency or circumstance was taken from them — no Service could be expected, none was attempted, the material in some degree is there, and the assurance already given, has rekindled the Hope of being again a corps worthy of the confidence of the Government.

There are six (6) revenue vessels on the Lakes, each about Fifty tons, too large for Custom House boats & too small for the service demanded of Cutters.

The cutters "Wm L. Marcy" and "Jefferson Davis" are on the Pacific Coast, fine vessels of one hundred and eighty tons each.

In one week there will be ready for any service — the Cutters "Morris", "C. Cushing", "Varina", "Crawford", "Campbell", & "Dobbin" — They were originally intended, as I understand it, for cooperating with the Army. I reported the fact to Genl. Patterson who directed me to place them where I considered they could perform the best service. As many changes have been made since, not only in transporting Troops but by a large addition of this kind of force by the Navy, I shall ask for further instructions; provided it meets with the sanction of the Department. I respectfully ask instructions on this point.[8]

While in Washington, he wrote five others letters to Chase, one stating that the *Varina* was ready to receive her officers, one stating again that *Philip Allen* was unworthy of arming and repairing, one recommending that the suspected slaver *Grapeshot* in New York be purchased for the $10,000 it would cost to repair *Philip Allen,* one naming officers for the *Varina,* and one recommending that two boards be established; one to examine Lieutenants in service, and one to examine applicants for commissions. In regard to the boards, he wrote:

"I would respectfully suggest a Board be appointed consisting of One Captain U.S. Rev Marine, one Lieutenant U.S. Navy and one Ship master of well known character, to examine the Lieutenents now in service, as to their qualifications as Seamen and Navigators. Also that a Board be convened for the examination of such applicants as the Hon Secretary of Treasury may designate."[9]

Chase did not go along with his desire to abandon *Philip Allen* and purchase *Grapeshot* but he did approve the establishment of one examining board (not two). Back in New York, Howard sent him a list of three men who had agreed to serve on the board. They were Revenue Cutter Captain Douglass Ottinger, who became President, Lieutenant E. C. Blake of the Navy, and Captain Jeff Maury of the Atlantic States Shipping Company. The board was established in June with an office at 240 Broadway, New York City,[10] a combination office building and hotel where Howard lived. Writing to Howard June 20, Captain Ottinger said:

"By an act of Congress approved March 2, 1855, 'that no person shall be appointed to the office of Captain, First, Second, or Third Lieutenant of any Revenue Cutter, who does not adduce competent proof of proficiency and skill in Navigation and Seamanship.'

Understanding from you that the above mentioned classes of officers will probably appear before this Board for examination, we respectfully submit the enclosed as a standard for their examination.

The Board in submitting the standard for First Lieutenant's examination do so with a view to their fitness for promotion to a Captaincy and therefore do not propose to make any different standard for Captains about to enter the Service."[11]

The Board soon ran into trouble. Men who had served as officers for many years balked at the idea of now being examined, especially since they were given short notice of examination dates. On July 10, Ottinger reported that the Board had great difficulty due to the failure to appear of candidates who had been ordered to take the examination. Some flatly refused. Others asked for a postponement and a leave of absence to study. One officer used "violent and disrespectful" language accusing the Treasury Department of dishonorable motives.

Of those who did finally consent to examination, many were found to be wanting in either seamanship or navigation, and were failed. They were not, however, dismissed from the service for by then Captain Howard was in desperate need of officers.

A further complication developed in August when Captain Maury presented a bill for $620 for 62 appearances at the Board at $10 each. The others received no extra pay for Board duty. Maury was paid $150 and dismissed. Revenue Cutter Captain Henry D. Hunter took his place.[12]

The proposed examination for Third Lieutenant consisted of two parts, one in Navigation, one in Seamanship. As originally designed, it read:

Examination for Third Lieutenant Entering the United States Revenue Service.

Navigation

Multiplication and Division by Logarithms Day's work
   Course and distance by Mercators Sailing
      Latitude by Meridian-Altitudes-Longitudes by chronometer (Sun's altitude) Distance given to find use of Mercator charts.
   Adjusting and use of Sextant and Quadrant

Seamanship

Rigging ship — Bending and unbending Sails
   General Management of a Ship in ordinary circumstances
Marking and use of hand and deep sea lead line"[13]

Before approving the examination, Chase wrote to the Superintendent of the Naval Academy at Newport asking, "Is this standard too high for the requirements of the law here cited?"[14]

All the officers and men were asked to take the oath of allegiance that summer. It read:

> "I do solemnly swear that I will support, protect, and defend the Constitution and Government of the United States against all enemies, whether domestic or foreign, and that I will bear true faith, allegiance, and loyalty to the same, any ordinance, resolution, or law of any State Convention or Legislation to the contrary notwithstanding, and further that I do this with the full determination, pledge, and purpose without any mental reservations or evasions whatsoever, and further that I will well and faithfully perform all the duties which may be required of me by law. So help me God."[15]

On most cutters, all willingly took the oath but on *Jackson*, moored off the Battery in lower Manhattan, there was trouble. When a Notary Public came on board September 5 to administer the oath, the officers took the oath "cheerfully", but 14 of the forward hands refused. Captain Amasa L. Hyde later placed the blame on one of his former Lieutenants, Isaac McKinley, who was much upset at that time by being required to take the disliked examination. When told that he would be arrested if he refused to be examined, Hyde said McKinley replied "Place me under arrest and be damned." Hyde called him a trouble-maker and said he had incited the forward hands who refused to take the oath. McKinley was later arrested and tried for his trouble-making. He was acquitted.

All 14 of the hands were kept in irons from September 5th to the 12th. The Notary returned on the 12th and all took the oath. Then they were discharged.[16]

The steamer *Bibb* was ready for service in June. She replaced the *Vixen* which went back to the Coast Survey. The *Bibb* was then stationed at Throggs Neck, an important station at the entrance to Long Island Sound from the East River, New York.

It was a busy Spring for Captain Howard. Of the 18 cutters in service when he took charge, one, the *Harriet Lane*, was transferred temporarily to the Navy, another, the *Walter B. Forward*, was serving the Army at Annapolis. Six Coast Survey vessels were added to the fleet, along with three steam tugs, *Reliance, Tiger* and *Hercules* at Baltimore, the chartered steamer, *General Sumner*, at San Francisco, and two yachts. This made a total of 30 vessels. *Cushing, Morris* and *Campbell* remained in New England. The *Dobbin* was stationed on the Delaware; the three tugs at Baltimore, the yachts on Long Island Sound and Baltimore, the *General Sumner, Marcy, Davis* and *Joe Lane* on the Pacific. By June the Coast Survey steamer *Bibb* had replaced the *Vixen* in New York. Others there were the *Crawford, Jackson, Varina, Agassiz* (which replaced the Coast Survey *Arago*) and the *Corwin*. On the Great Lakes some of the cutters had not been put back in the water when the lakes thawed. Collector G. W. Clason of Milwaukee may have reflected the views of other Collectors on the lakes when he wrote Chase saying:

As to the service of a Revenue Cutter on this lake, candor requires me to say that it affords no aid to commerce, and its *only* use seems to be to deplete the Treasury.[17]

Trouble Ahead

Howard began to have trouble with Customs Collector Barney in June. Barney questioned whether hammocks, bags, and flags that Howard had ordered were necessary, and delayed in sending necessary arms. He also questioned the need of the steamer *Bibb* at Throggs Neck. Howard answered by saying had she been there earlier, a traitor would not have escaped.[18]

Howard continued to ask that the *Philip Allen* be discarded and that the suspected slaver *Grapeshot* and another suspected vessel *Kate* be purchased for the service. Chase continued to turn a deaf ear. The *Allen* was thoroughly overhauled at the Philadelphia Navy Yard at great expense.

Marines on Board the Cutters

One of Captain Howard's innovations was the placing of ten "marines" on each of the cutters. These were not men from the United States Marines but enlisted men whose chief responsibility was defense of the cutters in time of trouble. They were drilled regularly on deck, or on shore, if possible. They were not highly popular with captains or crews, and in some instances were soon phased out. Each cutter also had a drummer and fifer on board.

The cutters in New York were constantly being shifted around, from Throggs Neck to the Narrows to Perth Amboy. In the summer *Bibb* was sent to guard the seaward approaches to New York at the Narrows when it was rumored that the rebels were about to attack Fort Lafayette where rebel prisoners were being held. For several days no vessels were permitted to leave the harbor, and Captain Ottinger was busy chasing those that tried to escape. He fired across the bows of several to make them come to and be examined. In one case, he had to fire at the vessel and the shots damaged her walking beam.[19]

Bibb was returned to the Coast Survey when Vice Admiral Fox of the Navy wanted her to assist in sinking the fleet of old whalers filled with stone at the entrance to Charleston. Her officers and men were shifted to other cutters. *Arago* and *Corwin* also went back to the Coast Survey, *Arago* being replaced by another Coast Survey vessel, *Agassiz*.[20] By the end of the year there were only three Coast Survey vessels in the Revenue Marine Service — *Varina*, *Crawford*, and *Agassiz*. They remained on guard duty throughout the war.

From April to August, the *Harriet Lane* was taking orders from Gideon Welles, Secretary of the Navy, Chase, Howard, and Barney, with Captain Faunce making most of the decisions, and the Revenue Marine Service paying most of the expenses. Some of the officers received no pay for months. In June, when the cutter returned to New York after convoying troops to the South, Howard wrote Chase that she needed better armament and asked permission to mount a suitable battery on her. Chase answered that he did not even know that the *Harriet Lane* had returned to New York, and he thought any expense in re-arming her should be paid by the Navy.[21]

When *Harriet Lane* was sent to Hampton Roads in June, she was directed to take orders from General Butler of the Army, but she was still a revenue cutter termporarily in the Navy. This must have been as puzzling to Captain Faunce as the status of the cutter *Forward* was to Captain Henry Nones. Nones was stationed at Annapolis under Navy orders to assist the Army. He felt he was obliged, and entitled to fly the national flag instead of the insignia of the Revenue Marine. For this he was severely rebuked by Army and Navy officers. Assistant Secretary Harrington wrote him saying:

> As you seem to have acted under a misapprehension, it will be sufficient to state that your vessel must at all times bear the revenue flag unless when formally transferred to the Navy Department when by law the Cutter is under the part of the naval force of the United States.

> Under your present orders, you are acting merely in conjunction with officers of the Army in carrying out the purposes of the government and hereafter you will fly the revenue flag unless specially authorized otherwise.[22]

"Who is Secretary, You or Mr. Chase?"

In June, the tone of Captain Howard's letters to the Treasury Department (especially to Harrington whom he had formerly addressed as "Friend Harrington") began to change. He now addressed him as "Sir." Both Chase and Harrington were questioning some of Howard's expenditures and methods.

On July 1, Harrington wrote him a lengthy letter saying that the Secretary required "system and economy" and he must know the exact cost of all items before he would give his sanction. No expensive repairs were to be undertaken before a survey had been made and an estimate given, and all expenses should be designated to individual cutters. He also felt that the Navy should pay for any changes in the *Harriet Lane.*

"In regard to officers," he continued, "you have ordered men hither and thither and given no notice and when we give orders we are met by some other having been given by you and thus the signature of the Secretary is called in question." He went on to say:

> "This has occurred two or three times. The question then arose who is Secy, you or Mr. Chase."[23]

He deplored the condition of the Revenue Marine Service and ended his letter saying:

> "It is not Pleasant nor can it go on so without creating difficulty. It excites remarks out of Washington & the officers don't seem to know what to do; such are the facts."[24]

Not long after, Captain Howard put an end to his friendly relations with the Treasury Department by embarking on an expensive and fruitless expedition without seeking the approval of the Secretary.

On July 11, a telegram from Newport, Rhode Island, was delivered to Collector Barney at the New York Custom House. It stated that a Confederate Privateer had captured a ship, two brigs and two schooners off the coast of New England. About the same time, an English ship arrived in port with news that she had narrowly escaped being seized by the same vessel. The story quickly appeared on the streets in the "New York Herald."[25]

Five Cutters Go to Sea

Having heard the news at 12:30 in the afternoon, Captain Howard sprang into action. Without notifying Secretary Chase, he ordered *Crawford, Varina, Jackson, Cushing, and Morris* to prepare for sea immediately. At 3:30, he himself was on board *Crawford,* and with *Varina* and *Jackson,* was towed down the harbor to Sandy Hook. Outside Sandy Hook, the cutters cast loose from the tug and drifted around in light airs until the following afternoon, when *Varina* and *Jackson* were ordered South, and the *Crawford* sailed East to rendez-vous with the New England cutters on the Nantucket shoals.

In a letter written July 12 to Chase, Howard said:

"Knowing full well the immense damage that might be done on our unarmed merchantmen in a very few days, I determined at once to proceed to sea with the Cutters in New York and Boston, hoping to destroy the vessel (brig) and give assurances on the part of Government to the Commercial Community their interest and safety were not neglected. Believing, firmly, that I could not do wrong in protecting the honor of the Government and the interest of the Citizens.[26]

When he joined *Cushing* and *Morris* on the Nantucket shoals, he sent the *Cushing* to the Grand Banks, the *Morris* to Sable Island along the track of the European vessels homeward bound. He wrote Chase:

"With a line of five vessels from Grand Banks to Hatteras I trust one of us may fall in with him (the pirate)."[27]

The Cutters had on board provisions only for July so Howard instructed them to return to port by August 1.

In his letter, he put in another plea for the purchase of *Grapeshot* and *Kate,* saying:

"May I take the liberty of stating to the Department that anticipating this Raid of Privateers and Slavers on our commerce, I solicited permission to purchase the "Grapeshot" and "Kate" (being notedly fast vessels) for outside cruisers as the Honl. Secretary did once favourably entertain the project I hope he will again give it his consideration."[28]

The search came to naught. The cutters had a pleasant summer cruise for two weeks, and with the exception of the *Jackson,* saw neither hid nor hair of Confederate activity. On July 16 on the North Carolina coast, Captain Hyde of the *Jackson* saw two wrecks being plundered by the British ship *Glory* of the Jersey Islands.[29] He thought the *Glory* had just come from Rio de Janeiro. Her Captain was communicating with a group on the beach bearing a British flag. They had several teams of horses, and a number of small boats. Captain Hyde sent an officer and boat's crew ashore with a flag of truce to investigate, but no one on shore or on the *Glory*, would communicate with them. The flag of truce was then withdrawn and the men returned to the *Jackson*. When the Captain saw a battery being set up on the beach, he opened fire with his big gun. The shots fell short but the men fled into the woods and sand hills and disappeared. Due to the shallowness of the water, the *Jackson's* guns could not reach the *Glory* or the beach, so Hyde left and continued south. On July 18th, he was off Cape Hatteras. In the Journal, he wrote:

> At 11:30 AM took a good look at Cape Hatteras and vicinity.[30]

He saw a vessel near Hatteras and gave chase until he discovered that she was inside the dunes in Albemarle Sound.

Captain Howard Leaves the Service

Howard's Revenue Marine days were numbered. On August 19 he was sent to Baltimore to take charge of the *Reliance* and fit out the other tugs, *Tiger* and *Hercules*. He advised Chase that 12-pounder rifle guns had been ordered for each of the tugs, and that they would require 12 minnie muskets, 12 pistols, 12 boarding pikes, and 12 cutlasses. He found that engineers could be hired in Baltimore at $50 and $60 a month for first engineers and $40 a month for assistants, plus rations. Each tug, he said, would require a Captain or Lieutenant in command, two other Lieutenants, a gunner's mate, two quartermasters, eight seamen, two boys, and ten marines. Each would also need a head engineer and assistant, two firemen, two coal passers, one cook, one steward, one ward room boy, and one pilot. He advised that crew be procured in New York since merchant ships in Baltimore were often detained for want of sailors.

On August 20, he was back in New York writing to Chase about uniforms. He said that the Revenue Marine Service uniforms were obsolete and that no two were alike.[32] He suggested that a board be appointed to study the matter.* He also sent the names of those who had recently taken examinations. Captain D. C. Constable was demoted to First Lieutenant. H. O. Porter, D. D. Tompkins, Thomas M. Dungan, and I. I. McKinley were promoted from Second to First Lieutenant. Five "gentlemen" who had dropped out of the service were reinstated. John McGowan passed the examination for Captain, and three Third Lieutenants - H. D. Hall, Frank Barr, and Morton Phillips were passed. H. H. Walsh, examined for Third Lieutenant, did so well he became a Second Lieutenant. Veteran Rufus Coffin failed to obtain a Captaincy because he had no knowledge of gunnery. Howard suggested that he be instructed and re-examined since he was a good sailor. Only a few (about one-fourth) appeared for the examinations.[33]

In October Howard was removed from New York and put in command of the cutter he despised — the *Philip Allen*. He was ordered to sail her to Havre de Grace, Maryland, where on October 27, he was visited by Assistant Secretary Harrington.[34] What happened at that meeting is not reported in letters or in *Allen's* journal, but two weeks later, Howard resigned from the Revenue Marine Service in order to join the Army. He became Colonel in the 1st New York Artillery, remaining in the Army until the end of the war, but changing to the 13th New York Heavy Artillery as a Colonel in 1863.

That was not the last that the Revenue Marine Service was to hear of William Howard. After the war, he was appointed by the United States Senate to inspect all the cutters on the Atlantic seaboard. Two years later he was put in charge of an expedition to Alaska on the new steam cutter *Lincoln*. He remained on special duty until 1870 when his health failed. He died in 1871.[35]

Franklin Pierce

PRESIDENT OF THE UNITED STATES OF AMERICA,

To all who shall see these presents, Greeting:

Know ye, That reposing special trust and confidence in the integrity, diligence, and good conduct of *John Faunce* I do appoint him *Captain* of a Cutter in the service of the United States, for the protection of the revenue; and do authorize and empower him to execute and fulfil the duties of that office according to law: And to have and to hold the said office, with all the rights and privileges thereunto legally appertaining, unto him, the said *John Faunce* during the pleasure of the President of the United States for the time being.

IN TESTIMONY WHEREOF, I have caused these letters to be made patent, and the seal of the Treasury Department of the United States to be hereunto affixed.

GIVEN under my hand, at the City of Washington, the *Eighth* day of *March* in the year of our Lord one thousand eight hundred and *fifty five* and of the Independence of the United States of America the *Seventy Ninth*.

By the President: *Franklin Pierce*

James Guthrie Secretary of the Treasury.

Commission of Captain John Faunce

CHAPTER VII

Captain Faunce and the Harriet Lane

Although the cutter *Harriet Lane* was temporarily transferred to the Navy April 5, 1861,[1] she remained under the command of Revenue Cutter Captain Faunce until she was sold to the Navy for $150,000 on September 11 of that year.[2] During the five month period from April to September which included two of the major sea battles of the Civil War, her officers and crew were all Revenue Marine personnel. Faunce took his orders from the Navy and the Army, but many decisions were made by the Revenue Service, the New York Customs Collector, and Faunce himself. The expenses were debated by both Treasury and Navy.[3]

Following the cutter's return from the unsuccessful attempt to reinforce Fort Sumter in April, Captain Faunce began several months of cruising in search of suspected vessels and convoying troops from New York to the Cheaspeake. Unfortunately, her journals for the war years are missing from the National Archives and the files of both the Treasury and Navy Departments. Fortunately, many of Faunce's letters to both departments remain to tell her remarkable story during the April-September 1861 period. Faunce was an able and prolific correspondent as well as a superior commander.

There were those who would belittle the *Harriet Lane*. For all her 180 feet, she was called "a small paddle-wheeler" by Navy critics. Captain David Dixon Porter USN once wrote:

"It shows the miserable condition of the Navy when the Department had nothing but a revenue cutter to depend on."[4]

However, the cutter could be depended upon to give a good account of her capabilities wherever she served, and Porter himself later chose her as his flagship during the Mississippi campaign in 1862.

Her junior officers in the April-September 1861 period included Revenue Cutter Second Lieutenant Henry O. Porter (brother of David Dixon Porter), Thomas M. Dungan, and Third Lieutenant Horace J. Gambrill. Both Porter and Gambrill had been on board the *Aiken* in Charleston when Captain Coste surrendered her to the South. Porter was to join the Navy and remain on the *Harriet Lane* in September. The other two lieutenants were later assigned to cutters in Baltimore.

A few days after she arrived from Sumter in April, the cutter was ordered to convoy the troop ship *Star of the West* from New York to the Potomac River. Faunce was instructed to "land and destroy any interfering batteries along the way," and, if the approach to Washington was "absolutely closed," to go to Annapolis. Faunce had no trouble in delivering the *Star of the West* and her priceless cargo to the Navy warship *Pocohontas* at the mouth of the Potomac.[5]

His next assignment was to proceed to the mouth of the Patapsco River, also on Cheasapeake Bay, and scrutinize all vessels leaving Baltimore. Secretary Welles had heard that there was a "movement on foot" to seize Navy transports and "other vessels on Government service." Faunce found no evidence of such a plot; indeed, he said, Baltimore was "strong for the Union."[6]

That spring, *Harriet Lane* was also ordered to accompany the fleet that transported the Naval Academy from Annapolis to war-time quarters at Newport, Rhode Island.[7] Faunce was temporarily relieved of command of the cutter May 13, 1861, but was back in command on June 7 when he was ordered by General Benjamin Butler of the Army to scout out enemy batteries on the James River. Here, on June 5, he drew fire from a hidden rebel post at Pig Point on the south side of Nansemond River. About 50 shots and shell were fired at the cutter, wounding five of his men. In a lengthy report to Flag Officer G. J. Pendergast, commander of the squadron at Fortress Monroe, Faunce described the action and commended his officers and men. This was headed:

> Reconnoissance by the U.S.S. Harriet Lane, Captain John Faunce, U.S. Revenue Marine, of Hampton Roads and vicinity, June 4, and an engagement with Confederate battery at Pig Point, Va., June 5, 1861.[8]

In his report he said:

> "Two of the shot took effect on the vessel, one passing through the plank-sheer forward of the fore rigging on the port side and out through the starboard bulwarks; the other through the fore rigging, grazing the foremast...Having accomplished my mission of drawing the fire of the enemy, and thereby discovering the strength of their battery, and finding the range of my guns less that theirs, after an engagement of forty-five minutes I drew off out of range."[9]

The five wounded were John Brainerd, Peter Woods, Chris Kane, Charles Johnson, and Nicolas Payne. Their wounds were superficial.[10]

In light of the circumstances it is hard to believe that Captain Faunce could be criticized as disloyal, but he was worried about rumors to that effect on

July 8 when he wrote Secretary Chase proclaiming that he was loyal. During the summer of 1861, he became acquainted with leading Army and Navy men. He won the approval of Captain Silas H. Stringham, commander of the Atlantic Blockading Squadron, when he boarded and chased away a suspected British vessel trying to enter a creek on Cape Charles. Stringham wrote Chase about this, and also said:

> "I have the honor to report some suggestions made to me by Capt. John Faunce of the "Harriet Lane" which I cheerfully endorse."[11]

Faunce had suggested that a revenue cutter be anchored at the Hog Island inlet and another in Chincoteague Inlet. He had told Stringham that there were several spare cutters at New York that might be used. No cutters, however, were ever stationed in the inlets.

Faunce had other plans for the Revenue Marine which he wrote in some detail to Secretary Chase asking that they be proposed to Congress to make the system more proficient.

On August 10, he was ordered by Stringham to leave Newport News and rendezvous with the United States frigate *St. Lawrence* which had just sunk the Confederate privateer *Petrel* off the coast of Georgia. He was to carry mail to the ships in the Blockading Squadron off Charleston and Savannah and bring back two witnesses to the sea battle.

Petrel, on her first raiding cruise out of Charleston, had mistakenly fired on *St. Lawrence* thinking she was a merchant ship. Return fire sank her in 30 minutes. Of the 38 rebels on board, 36 were rescued. The other two were drowned. The "pirates", as they were called, were all tried for piracy but latter acquitted.

Faunce returned to Chesapeake Bay August 20 bringing with him the two witnesses, a midshipman and a seaman from the *St. Lawrence.*[12]

On to Hatteras

Back in Hampton Roads, Faunce found a large fleet being assembled, under command of Flag Officer Stringham and Army General Benjamin Butler, to sail south. He also found that the *Harriet Lane* was to be part of the fleet which consisted of four Navy vessels, the chartered Navy steam transports *Adelaide* and *George Peabody* with 1,000 troops, the Navy tug *Fanny,* and over 200 surfboats. Many of the surfboats had been loaned by the Revenue Marine, having been gathered up at life-saving stations along the coast of Long Island. The transports towed schooners carrying surfboats; the *Monticello* and *Pawnee,* two of the warships, towed the surfboats themselves. The expedition left the Chesapeake, destination Hatteras Inlet, on August 25. Early in the morning of August 27, the red and white striped lighthouse at Cape Hatteras was in view, and at five P.M., the fleet anchored near shore and lowered the lifeboats in preparation for landing the troops the next morning.

There was a rough surf the next day but by noon, the surfboats had landed many of the men about two miles east of Fort Clark with *Harriet Lane, Pawnee,*

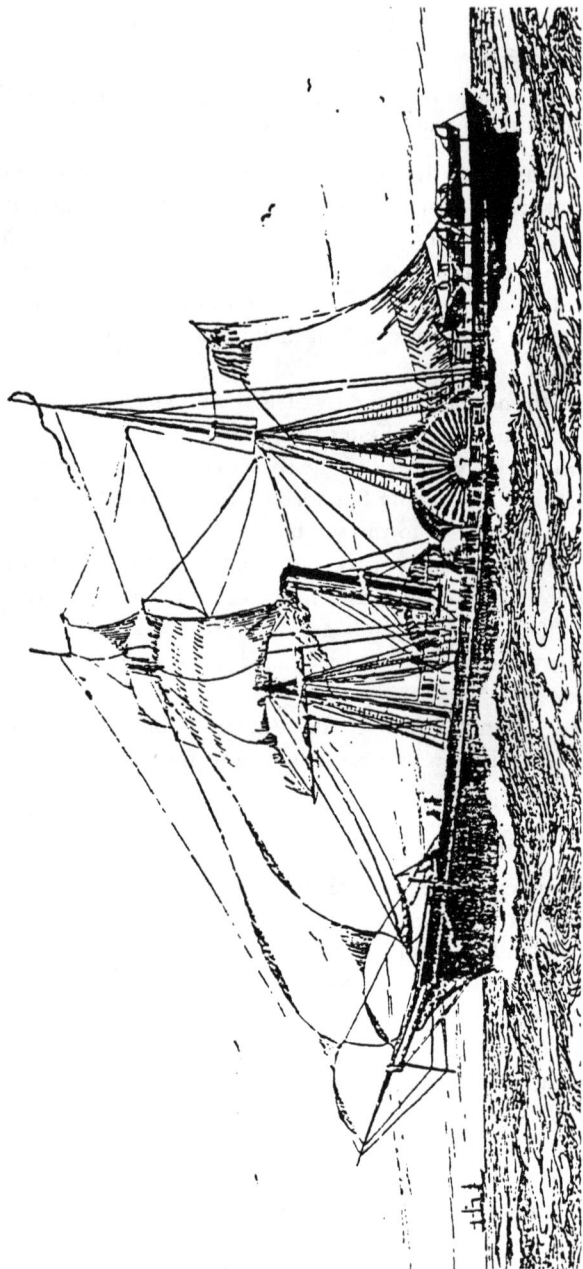

Cutter *Harriet Lane*

Tide Rips, 1934

and *Monticello* nearby to cover the landing. Meantime the other vessels attacked Fort Clark and Fort Hatteras, and received fire in exchange. The *Harriet Lane* was later commended for "good execution" with her rifled guns. At 12:30 P.M. the forts ceased firing and hauled down their Confederate flags.

Thinking that the rebels had surrendered, Stringham ordered the *Monticello* into the inlet. When she neared Fort Hatteras, there was gunfire from the Fort. The *Monticello* responded. By six P.M. the Fort ceased firing again and by noon the next day both forts had been abandonned. The tug *Fanny* was then sent into the inlet with the *Harriet Lane* behind her. The cutter had a good pilot on board, but she went aground on a shoal. She was able to back off without much difficulty. Faunce then went back to the flagship for another pilot whom he sent into the inlet in a small boat to explore the channel. While he was without a pilot he was ordered to proceed through the inlet. Although he protested that he had no pilot on board and that the *Harriet Lane* drew too much water to chance the inlet without a pilot, he was told to follow the *George Peabody*. He obeyed and at 1:15 P.M. found the vessel "took the ground." She was high and dry on a sand bar.

In his report later to Stringham, Faunce wrote:

"29th — When I found it was impossible to move the ship, for her preservation commenced lightening by throwing shot, shell, and coal overboard, and made every exertion to get her off; about 5 p.m. throwing the four 32 pounders over to windward. A boat came from the Susquehanna and was sent back with a request for more boats and men, which were sent by that vessel and also by the Pawnee. The engines began filling with sand from injection pipe, and the feed pumps having stopped, I was obliged to use the donkey pump to supply boilers. During the night kept all hands employed lightening ship, and made sail, endeavoring to make her beat over the shoal, but without effect, as we had no boat large enough to carry out an anchor in the sea then running."[13]

Having secured the forts with troops and taken command of the inlet after the Confederates signed a surrender, Stringham and most of the fleet went back to Chesapeake Bay leaving the *Harriet Lane* at the mercy of the sand and heavy seas of Cape Hatteras. There seemed to be little hope for the paddle-wheeler who had withstood tests at Paraguay and Sumter, and now met an enemy more deadly than South Americans and Confederates. On August 30th, Faunce wrote:

"30th — The ship labored heavily, lifting the engine frames. Found starboard air pump disabled; disconnected it, took off foot-valve bonnet, and worked starboard engine high pressure. At 8:30 a.m., the starboard boiler leaking badly, hauled fire, blew off water, shut stop valve, and used port boiler only. With the assistance of the Susquehanna's launch got out port bower, stream, and large kedge anchors, and at flood tide hove the ship about six times her length toward the channel. All hands at work throwing over spars, stores, provisions, etc."[14]

His chief engineer, Frank H. Pulsifer, also graphically described the desperate plight of the cutter in a letter home. He said, in part:

We lay there helpless for 48 hours and for the first 24 hours the sea wa making a clean breach over us. The *Lane* lay on her side and all tha saved us was that the seas hit the bottom of the vessel instead of the decks The small boats were all swamped. The steamer was bent and buckle(so that bolts were snapped off the bulkheads and the boilers were wrenche(so that is was impossible to make steam.[15]

Faunce spent another sleepless night trying to save the cutter he had helpe(to build and had commanded ever since she first hit the water. The next after noon, at 2:20 P.M. she began to move. He wrote:

"31st — Hauled fire in port boiler, and blew off water and steam, to lighter ship. At 2:20 p.m., after laboring nearly fifty hours, succeeded in haul ing the vessel off the shoal. Steam tugs *Fanny* and *Tempest* took her ir tow, and at 3:30 came to anchor in Hatteras inlet, off Fort Hatteras."[1]

He remained at Hatteras until September 4, making temporary repair and taking on seven tons of coal from the *Pawnee*. The cutter was in runninɡ order at 6 A.M. on the 4th, and back at Hampton Roads September 6.

Five days later, Treasury Secretary wrote the following letter to G. V. Fox Acting Secretary of the Navy:

"I have the honor to transmit herewith the papers necessary to the per manent transfer of the Rev Steamer "Harriet Lane" to the Navy Dep as required by law. I will thank you to cause a requisition to issue fot the amount of the enclosed account, directing the same to be coverec into the Treasury by Counter Warrant as a miscellaneous receipt to b(refunded to the appropriation for a suitable Steamer or Rev Cutter ir accordance with 5 Section of Act of Congress of 25 July 1861.

The officers and men of the "Harriet Lane" will be detached withou delay."[17]

He enclosed a message from President Lincoln written September 2, saying

"By virtue of authority rested in me under the 5 Section of an Act of Con gress entitled an "Act relative to the Revenue Marine, to fix the compen sation of the officers thereof and for other purposes" approved 25 July 1861, I hereby transfer permanently to the Navy, the Steamer "Harrie(Lane" heretofore belonging to the Revenue Cutter Serivce."[18]

Plans for the sale of the cutter to the Navy had already gone through wher she was struggling to free herself from the Hatteras sand. She was sold fot $150,000, the sum to be used to purchase "a suitable steamer or Rev Cutter"[19] for the service President Lincoln now called the "Revenue Cutter Service." The deal went through, marked

Approved

Abraham Lincoln[20]

It must have been a sad day for Captain Faunce when he heard the news. Having commanded the cutter since she was launched in February 1858, and having just saved her from being torn to shreds in Hatteras currents, he was now ordered to sail her to the Philadelphia Navy Yard and turn her over to the command of Commander J. M. Wainwright, USN.

The cutter, once the pride of the Revenue Marine, was in deplorable condition as she limped up the Delaware to the Navy Yard. All her guns and ammunition had been thrown into Davy Jones' locker, along with a tank of quicksilver, crank pins, bolts, 12 bars of iron, 100 pounds of white lead, 100 pounds of red lead, tallow, paint, broken furniture, 1,080 salt rations, 50 pounds of beef and countless personal belongings. Her officers and crew were in rags — and penniless. They had received no pay for nine months due to a dispute between the Navy and the Revenue Marine.[21]

When the officers went ashore to the Girard Hotel in Philadelphia, they were turned away because they did not have any money, but they were received with open arms at the more patriotic Hotel Continental. A few days later they all received their 9 months' back pay — from the Revenue Marine, not the Navy.[22]

Much of *Harriet Lane's* furniture went into storage to be used two years later on the *Cuyahoga*. Captain Faunce then left for Hoboken, New Jersey, where he supervised the commissioning of the first ironclad of the Revenue Marine Service, the *Naugatuck*, soon to be renamed *E. A. Stevens* for her builder. It would be six years before he would see *Harriet Lane* again, and then under quite different circumstances.[23]

CHAPTER VIII

New Problems for the Revenue Marine

In its new role as Jack and Jill of all trades, the Revenue Marine ran into some unusual problems. Take the case of the *Tiger*, the Baltimore steam tug bought from the Patapsco Steam Tug Company in August 1861 for $9,000.[1] Put in commission and commanded by Captain McGowan, she hunted rebel vessels in Chesapeake Bay for a month and was then turned over to Captain Hyde to cruise along the Eastern Shore of Maryland with the two other deep draft steam tugs, *Reliance* and *Hercules*.

On November 13, the Navy steamer *Pocohontas*, with 1,000 troops on board, went aground in Tangier Sound. It took all three tugs to get her afloat. *Tiger* supplied her with water for the troops and towed her back to her squadron late that night. A week later she was assigned to escort *Pocohontas*, with cavalry on board, from Annapolis to Fortress Monroe. Returning to Baltimore she seized a rebel at Smiths Island and took him and his belongings to the city. Then she was ordered by the Baltimore Customs Collector to proceed to New York via the canals.[2]

The very next day, November 30, at 6:30 A.M. she "got underway and stood out of the Harbor to proceed to New [York] via the canals." There were two canals to negotiate—the Delaware and Chesapeake Canal between Chesapeake Bay and the Delaware River, and the Raritan Canal between Bordentown and New Brunswick, New Jersey.

Tiger "Takes the Bottom"

Even before she entered the Elk River leading to the Delaware and Chesapeake Canal, *Tiger* "took the bottom." That was at 11:30 A.M. Captain Hyde managed to get her off but by 2:45 P.M. she was aground again. Deep in the mud at the entrance to Back Creek, she now needed the help of another tug to set her free. At 5:30 P.M. she entered the canal. Half an hour later she was hit by a schooner which carried away her "signal poles, fish davit and starboard catheads." About four miles into the canal she went aground again. It was now 10:30 P.M. so the engineer shut down steam and everyone slept until morning.[3]

Between 7 and 9 A.M. the next morning she was on and off the bottom several times. "Finding it impossible to start either ahead or astern" Captain Hyde ordered the water blown out of her boiler and sent for a tow boat and a canal pilot. At 4 P.M. they entered the locks at Delaware City but since it was low water in the Delaware it was 7 P.M. before they could enter the river. The next day, December 2, they anchored near the Revenue Cutter *Dobbin* at the Philadelphia Navy Yard and Captain Hyde went ashore to consult on conditions in the Raritan Canal. Meantime *Dobbin* dragged into *Tiger* but no major damage was done. A pilot came aboard *Tiger* and they steamed up the Delaware in the night to Bordentown where they were to get a towboat from the Philadelphia-New York Propeller Company. At 4 A.M. they prepared to enter the locks of the canal. All guns and heavy gear was transferred to the towboat, the *Black Diamond*. At 5:30 A.M. December 4, the *Black Diamond* took them in tow and the canal voyage began.[4]

It lasted one-half hour. At 6 A.M. *Tiger* took the bottom again and refused to budge. More heavy gear was thrown off and kedge anchors were brought out. Three other steamers tugged and pushed but *Tiger* would not move. Late in the day Captain Hyde sent an officer to Bordentown to hire another steamer. He found none available. Desperate efforts to push the cutter forward were made again the next day. Captain Hyde finally gave up. He sent Lieutenant Constable to Washington to report to Secretary Chase, with a letter saying:

> I have the honor to report that in accordance with orders from the Collector of Customs of Baltimore to proceed with this vessel to New York through the Canals, that I have progressed thus far (Bordentown) but am unable to proceed further in consequence of lack of water in the Canal.
>
> I have dispatched Lieut. Constable to explain the facts of the case and give any explanation in regard to the vessel which the Asst. Secretary may require.[5]

The captain then ordered the *Black Diamond* to tow the cutter back to the Delaware River. She went aground again in the Delaware River at 10 o'clock that night.[6]

Back at the Philadelphia Navy Yard the next day, *Tiger* went into drydock. She had her propeller and shaft unshipped, and empty water casks lashed to her bottom for flotation. After four days in drydock she was floated and although lightened by five tons, was found to draw only six inches less than she had originally drawn.[7] Captain Hyde then went to Washington himself to seek advice. When he returned two days later the Philadelphia Customs

Collector ordered a survey of the vessel. As a result she went into the screw dock and all hands were put to work lashing on more empty water casks.

When she returned to the canal December 13, she was towed through "without incident," reaching Trenton at 6 A.M., Princeton at 11:30 A.M., Kingston at 5 P.M., and the Raritan River at New Brunswick at 9 P.M. Here she was taken in tow by the steamer *Weehauken* and hauled into the Atlantic Dock at Brooklyn where she "made fast alongside of an English ship."[8]

Hyde was exonerated, although criticized by men at the Philadelphia Navy Yard. He fastened the blame on the people who told him there was a nine-foot depth of water in the Raritan Canal, and that if he made it through the Delaware and Chesapeake Canal he could get through the Raritan Canal.[9]

It had taken *Tiger* 19 days to make the voyage from Baltimore to New York but make it she did! Once back in shape she relieved the steam cutter *Bibb* at the Narrows in New York Harbor. On her first day on duty she chased an English brig down the bay and had to fire a blank cartridge across her bow to bring her to. That day she boarded 20 vessels, 10 of them American, 8 of them British, 1 Russian and 1 Spanish.

In February Captain Rufus Coffin took command of the cutter. He liked to cruise around the harbor "under easy steam." In March *Tiger* left The Narrows and was ordered to stand guard at Perth Amboy to prevent goods from being smuggled on board vessels bound for the South. Captain Frances Martin took command when Captain Coffin was ordered to Port Royal, South Carolina that month.

Tiger was ordered to Washington in December 1862 but NOT through the canals. She went the long deep way around. Even so she managed to go aground twice, once off Cape May, and again near Baltimore.[10]

At Washington in 1863, under command of Captain John Jones, she was used to transport officials (and the unofficial Kate Chase) up and down the Potomac. In mid-June when Washington feared an invasion by the rebels she was stationed near the Washington Navy Yard. As her Journal said:

> Anchored off the Navy Yard to assist in protecting the City in the event of an attack by the Rebels. Moored ship in a position to command the Navy Yard bridge and the Roads leading thereto."[11]

She remained in the service at Washington and Baltimore until she was sold July 10, 1865 at Baltimore for $1,950. Her gear was transferred to the *Reliance*, the *Nemaha* and the *Jackson*.[12]

Yachtsmen Offer to Help

Soon after rebel guns fired on Fort Sumter several yachtsmen offered their yachts and their services to the Union. At a special meeting of the board of directors of the New York Yacht Club at the Breevort House on April 30 the annual regatta and cruise were cancelled and it was proposed to inscribe the following motion in the minutes:

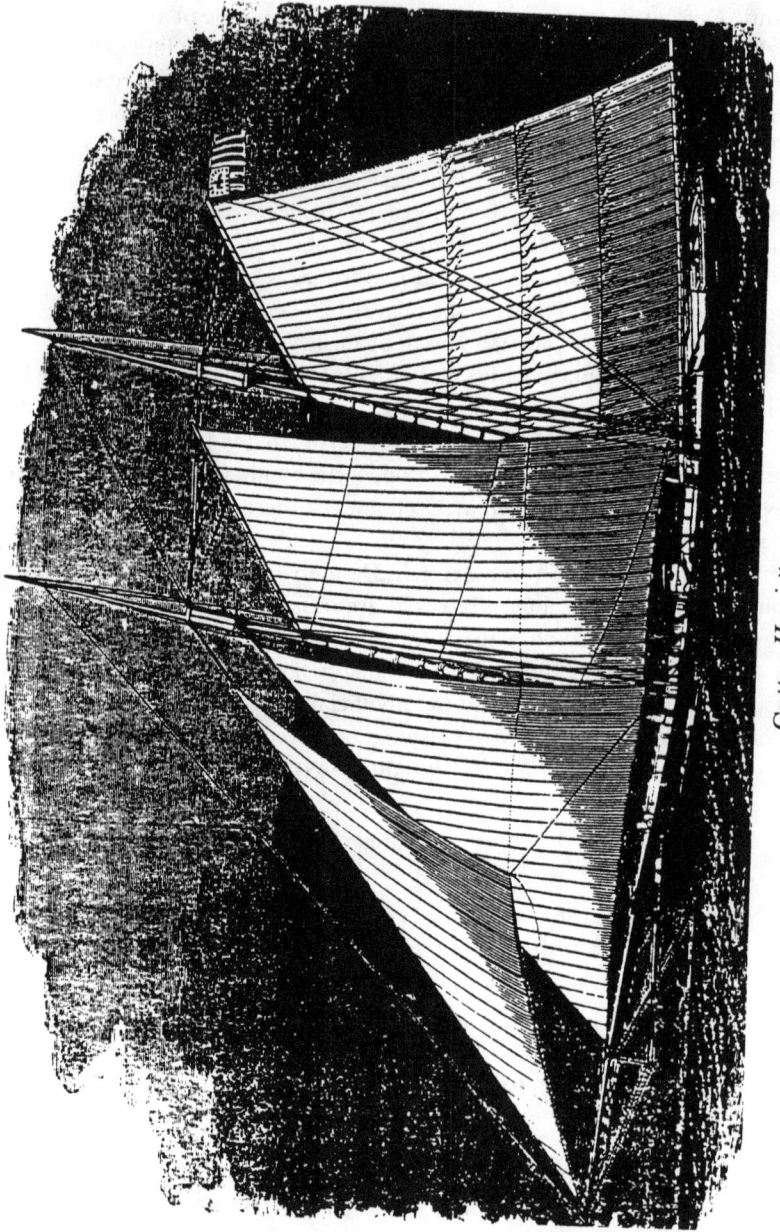

Cutter *Henrietta*

Harper's Weekly

The members of the New York Yacht Club resolve to offer, through the Commodore, the services of all their yachts for any duty compatible with the qualities and dimensions of their yachts.[13]

Two of the club's 52 schooners and sloops were taken into the Revenue Marine. Others may have been offered and rejected. Captain Howard was opposed to accepting any yachts, saying he believed "the service of the yachts generally would not justify the expenses attending their arming, manning and subsisting." However, one young yachtsman, 20-year old James Gordon V. Bennett Jr., son of the famous New York publisher, went directly to Secretary of State Seward and offered his new 158-ton fore-and-aft rigged schooner *Henrietta*. She was a fast keel boat, 92 feet long, with a clipper bow.

Seward referred him to Lincoln who then asked Secretary Chase to grant him an interview, saying that he tendered "a fine yacht of 160 tons to the U. S. Service."[14] Chase accepted not only *Henrietta* but another New York Yacht Club schooner, *Hope*, belonging to Thomas Boynton Ives, whose home port was Providence. Both men were commissioned Lieutenant Commanders and allowed two non-commissioned officers, ten seamen and $353 a month for each vessel. They were expected to furnish their own servants. The yachts were armed in New York by Captain Howard, and dispatched in July, *Henrietta* to Long Island and Nantucket, and *Hope* to Baltimore.

In his letter of instruction July 12 to Commander Bennett of the "U.S. Rev. Yacht *Henrietta*" Howard said:

"As soon as you have received your armament shot and shell you will please proceed with the U.S. Rev Yacht "Henrietta" under your command along the North Shore of Long Island to Block Island and Nantucket touching in all the ports (intermediate) calling on the different Collectors reporting yourself and Vessel ready to perform any duties required of you as Commander of a Rev Cutter in the service of the United States. You will obtain all the information in your power respecting the fitting out of Slavers and other illicit trade, permitting no vessel to pass having on board arms and munitions of war unless she is in the service of the United States, keeping a Journal of that and all passing events. On your return you will visit all the intermediate ports on the South Shore of the Main Land to New York, *boarding* and examining all vessels not known to be regular and honest traders.

On your return to New York you will present to the Collector of Customs of the Port a *transcript* of the Journal of your cruise with such remarks and information you may deem necessary to the public service.

You will during your cruise exercise your men daily (when the weather and duties of the Vessel will permit) at the Great Guns & small arms. Practice them once a week with shot and shells to the extent (in all) of twenty rounds per week.

You will keep a strict "Lookout" night and day examining every vessel that has the least suspicious appearance, enforcing a strict discipline in the event of being called upon to more active and important Service. You will ascertain the speed and trim of your Vessel under different canvass *by and large* noting the best points in your Journal.

Altho important powers and duties are confided to you, you will please exercise them in as pleasant and agreeable manner as possible, not detaining

an honest trader a moment longer than necessary to prevent fraud upon the
Revenue as also just to the fair and honest trader.

Wishing your a pleasant Cruise

I am, dear sir, very respectfully,

Your obdt Servant

W. A. Howard

Senior Captain[15]

A third yacht, *Zouave,* was tendered to the government by two brothers,
Benjamin and J. M. Wilson of Mystic, Connecticut, July 18, 1861. Collector Barney was authorized to receive her if he thought she was suitable. Captain Howard traveled to Mystic to look her over. He reported it would cost
too much to put her in condition and she was declined August 20. She is,
however, listed among the Revenue Cutters of 1861.[16]

The De Bebian Affair

No Journals of *Henrietta* have been located so it can only be assumed that
she did as told and proceeded to Block Island and Nantucket late in July and
was probably on her way back to New York when she met the schooner *Adelso*
which had put into Newport due to bad weather August 13.

Adelso had a peculiar history. She was a 98-ton vessel, built in Eastport,
Maine and originally owned by John Kay of Eastport who named her *A.L.
Hyde* in honor of Revenue Cutter Captain Hyde. Hyde was then in command
of the cutter *Jackson* at Eastport. Kay was in trade between Nova Scotia and
the South. When war broke out he found it expedient to turn the schooner
over to his brother-in-law, Henry Horton, a resident of New Brunswick who
registered her in New Brunswick and changed her name to *Adelso.* She sailed
under Captain Thomas Kimball, a naturalized American citizen born in Bri-
tain. She was then chartered for trade between Nova Scotia and North
Carolina. In spite of the blockade of Wilmington, North Carolina, she had
sailed in and out of that port and was bringing a full cargo of turpentine and
rosin to Boston when she ran into bad weather off Newport.[17]

Obeying Captain Howard's orders, 20-year old Lieutenant Commander
Bennett boarded *Adelso* and seized her on the strength of her dubious history,
the British connections of her master, and her defiance of the Atlantic
blockade. The vessel was searched and although no contraband was found
in the cargo, the trunks and personal effects of a passenger, Louis de Bebian,
yielded suspicious evidence of collaboration with the enemy.[18]

Officers of *Adelso* were to claim that their schooner was taken possession
of by "men armed to the teeth." Bennett, it was said, was "in martial panoply
with drawn sword, several revolvers and all his followers similarly accoutred."
The cutter's men held *Adelso* by order of the Newport Customs Collector Seth
W. Macy. No one was allowed to go ashore and all papers found on board
were sealed up.[19]

Four days later De Bebian was permitted to land and state his case.
Although he argued that he was innocent of any wrong doing, it was soon
evident that he was guilty of espionage. De Bebian was a native of Guadeloupe

and a citizen of France who had engaged in transporting lumber from the West Indies to Wilmington, defying the blockade. He alleged that his passage on *Adelso* was purely for commercial reasons but his trunk contained letters and papers showing that he was to purchase $40,000 worth of goods in Liverpool to be delivered in a British or French vessel to Confederate interests in Wilmington. The goods included between 5,000 and 10,000 army blankets, 1,000 bags of coffee, several tons of iron, and various articles of clothing. De Bebian claimed that the goods ordered were for citizens of North Carolina, saying that it was customary to provide a pair of blankets for each negro in the Fall. These he called "negro blankets."[20]

Further evidence against him included letters from Confederate sympathizers in Vermont, Maine, New York, Missouri and Connecticut. Nor did it help his case when Commander Bennett found complete instructions on how to run the blockade when entering Wilmington. Once a vessel gave the proper signal a pilot would be sent from shore to guide her to the city.

Collector Macy ordered De Bebian's arrest August 19. He was sent to Fort Lafayette at the Narrows in New York Harbor where he was held in custody until October 4 when he was permitted to leave for Europe. He was back in Wilmington in February where he was interviewed by the Wilmington, North Carolina Journal. The editor said he called Bennett "squint-eyed" and claimed he was a "bibulous youth who is the owner of a yacht in which he used to cruise around in the vicinity of Newport." The editor added:

> He tendered the yacht to the U. S. government as a cutter or something or other, on condition of his getting a commission as her commander, although he hardly knew one rope from another, having proceeded to secure the services of a real seaman to work the vessel.[21]

Bennett was ordered to Port Royal in February 1862 to assist the blockading squadron. When *Henrietta* sailed into port she was mistaken for a blockade runner until her Revenue Marine ensign was seen. Bennett was lavish in entertaining officers of the blockading squadron aboard his yacht. He returned north in April, being frequently mistaken for a blockade runner and chased several times along the way. By then young Bennett decided he had had enough of Revenue Marine life. He withdrew *Henrietta* April 29, 1862, and asked that she be returned to her former condition.[22]

After the war *Henrietta* became famous when she won the transatlantic race in 1866. Her young commander was later commodore of the New York Yacht Club, one of the youngest in its history.[23]

Hope Goes to Baltimore

Lieutenant Commander Ives set out from New York in his armed yacht, *Hope,* July 5 and ran into head winds and calms. It was the 13th before he reached Baltimore late at night. The next day he reported to the Baltimore

Collector, and was appalled at conditions in the harbor. On August 3 he wrote Secretary Chase saying:

> I found that up to that date [July 14] nothing whatever had been done to prevent vessels from leaving the Port at any and all times and that after they left the dock no measures were taken to ascertain of what their cargo consisted.[24]

Ives, in cooperation with the Collector, began issuing orders as soon as he arrived. He insisted that vessels clear coastwise, but, at the Collector's suggestion, gave permanent papers to local traders if they were "good and true men." They then had merely to report to the *Hope* as they passed out of the harbor. All other vessels were visited by *Hope's* officers. By the first of August they boarded 150 vessels.[25]

This, however, applied only to sailing vessels. Steamboats were supposed to have been thoroughly inspected before sailing. Writing to Chase, Ives said:

> As it would be a very great detention for steamboats to be stopped and examined by us here as they passed owing to the great facilities which their peculiar contruction and arrangement of their cabins present for smuggling, we arranged we would have nothing whatever to do with the steamboats but confine ourselves to sailing vessels and that Inspectors from the Custom House should be in constant attendance night and day on such vessels from the time of their arrival until their departure.[26]

Nevertheless he was soon ordered by General John Dix to board and examine the steamer *Mary Washington* bound for the Patuxent River. She had been detained at Fort McHenry on suspicion of carrying goods for Virginia. He and his men found three trunks, belonging to three lady passengers filled with military buttons, and a large dry goods box of military buttons and buckles. The trunks and the box had been put aboard just before the vessel sailed. The contraband was seized and the *Mary Washington* was allowed to proceed.

The next day General Dix ordered Ives to examine the *George Weems*, another passenger steamer. Eighty colt navy pistols, about 40,000 percussion caps and a third of a barrel of quinine in bottles, were found secreted on board. A number of percussion caps were also found aboard a schooner bound for St. Mary's City on the Potomac.

Within two weeks Ives had boarded about 39 vessels a day. He and his men had worked from sunrise to sunset, and felt they needed help. Ives suggested to Chase that they be given an inspector who knew how to handle small boats. He said some of the inspectors he had met were "good men" but did not know how to take the tiller. He also asked Chase for a boarding net for *Hope*, saying:

> She is not safe in these waters without one

He figured that 100 fathoms of small chain should be woven into the netting "to prevent its being cut with a cutlass or knife." This would cost about $50, bringing the cost of the net to an estimated $116.70.[27]

Whether Ives got his boarding net or not is not known. *Hope* remained in the Chesapeake only until October 11 when she was ordered to New York. By then Ives had had enough of the Revenue Marine Service. On November 4 he asked to withdraw with his yacht from the service. Four days later she was decommissioned.[28]

The *Cruiser* and the *Joe Miller*

Two small vessels, a schooner and a sloop, which may have been yachts, were chartered in Chesapeake Bay in September 1862 to assist the Revenue Marine. Both were commanded by Lieutenant Daniel D. Tompkins of the Revenue Marine. Their logs are in the National Archives but neither is listed in official Revenue Marine records.

The *Joe Miller's* journal, three sheets of London stationery sewed together and now browned and frayed, was signed by her commander and Captain McGowan of the cutter *Reliance*. The title reads:

> Abstract of the Journal of the U.S. Rev. Sloop *Joe Miller*. Daniel D. Tomp-kins, Lieut. Com'd'g. From Sept 3rd to Sept 11th, 1862 inclusive[29]

Joe Miller had four in crew. She stood down Chesapeake Bay September 2, sailing day and night in search of canoes suspected of carrying contraband. At 3 A.M. she was off Sharps Island. At 10:30 P.M. that night she was anchored off Fog Point Light in Kadges Straits where, early the next morning, she saw rocket signals fired from a boat in the Bay. Communicating with the keeper of the Fog Point Light she found that canoe traffic was frequent between the Eastern Shore and Virginia. She chased several canoes but could not catch them. Those she did stop proved to be legitimate local vessels out fishing.

On September 8 she met the cutter *Reliance* and was given a captured boat and two prisoners to be taken to Annapolis. While underway in a heavy sea the towed boat surged into her and tore away a part of her stern. She then had to put into the South River, below Annapolis, and make repairs. At Annapolis she delivered the boat to the cutter *Hercules* and took the two prisoners to the Marshall's office where they took the oath of allegiance to the United States and were given their freedom.

The Annapolis Collector ordered Tompkins to survey the damage to the *Joe Miller* and it was decided to return her to her owner, who agreed to repair her at his own expense. The Collector then authorized Tompkins to "engage another vessel at the same rate at which the *Miller* had been employed."

On September 11, Tompkins went on board the schooner *Cruiser* "having negotiated with the owner thereof for her charter." The *Cruiser's* journal is headed:

> Abstract of the Log of the U.S. Rev. Schr. "Cruiser" Daniel D. Tompkins Lieut. commanding from Sept. 12th to Sept. 30th 1862, both inclusive."

The two prisoners, having sworn their allegiance, were brought on board *Cruiser* and their boat was taken in tow, "the priviledge having been granted by the Marshall and Collector to take them home, also their boat and some things for family use." They were dropped off in Kadges Strait to sail for home.

Off Annemessex River, *Cruiser* met the cutter *Reliance*, Commander McGowan, and the two commanders conferred. Later, off Tangier Island, several canoes were boarded, and one, with three men on board, was seized. Tompkins took the men on board and dispatched two seamen to sail the canoe to Baltimore. Tompkins then sailed to Baltimore, turned the prisoners over to the District Attorney and filed a libel against the canoe.

Going down the Bay again, they stopped several canoes, sloops and pungies, all on legitimate business. One large canoe from the western shore was suspect until the captain produced a pass from the U.S. Military Authority of the Eastern Shore stating that he and his family were going to live in Annemessex. They watched *Reliance* seize a pungy but seized no vessels themselves before it was time to return to Baltimore. Going up the Bay, they met the steam tug *Spy* towing two government transports with troops. They found that an engineer on *Spy* had dislocated his shoulder in a fall. They took him on board for Baltimore, arriving there off Fells Point that night. *Cruiser* then went back to her owner.[31]

James K. Polk

PRESIDENT OF THE UNITED STATES OF AMERICA,

To all who shall see these presents, Greeting:

Know ye, *That reposing special trust and confidence in the integrity, diligence, and good conduct of* Douglass Ottinger. *I do appoint him* Captain *of a Cutter in the service of the* United States, *for the protection of the revenue; and do authorize and empower him to execute and fulfil the duties of that office according to law.: And to have and to hold the said office, with all the rights and privileges thereunto legally appertaining unto him the said* Douglass Ottinger *during the pleasure of the President of the United States for the time being.*

IN TESTIMONY WHEREOF, *I have caused these letters to be made patent, and the seal of the Treasury Department of the United States to be hereunto affixed.*

GIVEN *under my hand, at the City of Washington, the twenty-fourth day of December in the year of our Lord one thousand eight hundred and forty six - and of the Independence of the United States of America the seventy first*

By the President: J. K. Polk

R. J. Walker Secretary of the Treasury.

Commission of Captain Douglas Ottinger
National Archives

CHAPTER IX

The Chilly Voyage of Captain Ottinger

The people of Quebec found it hard to believe. Who was this strange American who arrived at night, with a fleet of five small schooners, and insisted on leaving the next morning for Boston? The wind was "blowing strong and the snow falling fast." It was the first of December, and there was already much ice in the river. Soon it would be frozen from shore to shore.

The five small schooners were revenue cutters from the Great Lakes headed for Civil War duty on the Atlantic, and the American was Captain Douglass Ottinger of the United States Revenue Marine who had been ordered by Treasury Secretary Chase to deliver the cutters as soon as possible. Chase needed them to replace the larger cutters now on duty with the Army and Navy.[1]

On August 13, his assistant, George Harrington, had written Collector Hiram Barney at New York saying:

> "I will thank you to ascertain whether it is practicable by _____ the _____ to transfer the six Revenue Cutters now on the lakes to the coast by canal. These vessels are about 50 to 55 tons. If not practicable by Canal, what probable expense would be by way of the St. Lawrence. Capt. Ottinger can give you the length, beam and draft of water, and it is presumed all necessary information in regard to them other than the cost of transportation."[2]

The cutters at Quebec were five of six centerboard schooners which had been built at the Merry and Gay Shipyard in Milan, Ohio in 1856, and stationed at leading ports on the Lakes. They averaged about 58-60 tons and were approximately 63 feet long and 17 feet wide. With the centerboard down they drew 12 feet; with it up almost six feet.[3]

Barney informed Harrington that it would be impossible to bring the center-board vessels through the Erie Canal. Ottinger was then asked to give an estimate of the cost of moving five vessels from their stations on Lakes Michigan, Huron, St. Clair, Erie, and Ontario via the St. Lawrence River to some American port on the Atlantic. The sixth cutter *John D. Floyd* was to remain on Lake Superior.

On October 6, Ottinger, then President of the Revenue Marine Service Examining Board in New York City, answered the "Honorable" Harrington as follows:

> In compliance with your direction I respectfully submit to you the following estimate of expenses and time necessary to move the Revenue vessels from Lakes Michigan, Huron, St. Clair, Erie, and Ontario.[4]

For the cutter *Aaron V. Brown* stationed at Milwaukee he gave the following estimate:

From Milwaukee to Lake Erie towage	$200
Towage through Welland and St. Lawrence Canals	88
Pilotage from Montreal to sea	50
Wages for 4 seamen 1 month	120
Wages for one cook	28
Rations for five men one month	37.50
	$523.50[5]

For the *Isaac Toucey* stationed at Michilimackinac, the total would be somewhat less, $423.50. It would cost only $100 to tow her to Lake Erie. For the *Jacob Thompson* at Detroit, it would be $338.50, with towage at $15, and for the other two cutters, *Jeremiah S. Black* and *Howell Cobb*, with no towage necessary, it would be $323.50 and $313.50. It would cost ten dollars less to tow the *Howell Cobb*, smallest in the fleet, through the canals.[6]

Ottinger went on to discuss the time element. He said:

> "The time necessary to move the above mentioned Revenue schooners from their present stations to Boston or New York would be about five weeks. If only those at Detroit, Erie, Penna., and Oswego, N. York are needed to be moved one week less time would be sufficient. The navigation on the Lakes is considered extra hazardous after the 15th of November. There would probably be incidental expenses of sixty (60) dollars for each Cutter exclusive of the estimates as detailed."[7]

In his estimates, Ottinger was expecting that Revenue Marine Service officers would be detailed to command each cutter. He recommended Lieutenants Edward Freeman of Boston, Vancuel Colesbury and Timothy Treadway of Philadelphia, John G. Baker of Cleveland, and Daniel Tompkins and Thomas M. Dungan of New York. If five of these officers were assigned, he said, he need not engage masters from the Merchant Marine.[8]

Chase inquired about Ottinger and was told by Collector Barney that he was a "useful officer," especially in the capacity of an examiner. He would be missed on the examining board but his place could be taken by Captain John McGowan.[9]

As weeks went by, Ottinger grew increasingly nervous about the ice conditions on the lakes. At last he was assigned and dispatched. On October 18, Chase ordered him to get the cutters to the Atlantic "as soon as possible after this letter is received." The letter did not arrive until October 22. Ottinger left immediately for Milwaukee where he found the cutter *Aaron V. Brown* already in winter storage on the Menominee River.

Since no Revenue Marine officers had been engaged to assist him, he was obliged to engage a master and mate, as well as four seamen and cook for each cutter. Writing to Chase October 23, he repeated his warning that navigation on the Lakes was dangerous after November 15 and that he was afraid of being frozen in before the expedition could be got underway. There would also be ice in the Canadian canals late in November.

Chase had hoped to eliminate towage fees, but Ottinger assured him towage was necessary so late in the season. Freight rates and seamen's wages were going up as vessels hurried to complete deliveries before the ice came. Wages, he told Chase, had increased 25% since the first of October.
He wrote:

> It is not probable that I can carry your order into effect without incurring the expense for towage, as per estimate, as it will be necessary for me to avail myself of every means of dispatch to escape being frozen in; I shall keep in mind, as you direct, your wishes respecting a rigid economy.

> One thousand dollars will be the sum that I shall need in hand. Please instruct the Collector at this port by telegraph to advance to me that sum.[10]

A Voyage of 2,325 Nautical Miles

With the help of Collector E. Brown at Milwaukee, Captain Ottinger got the *Brown* out of winter storage and re-rigged her for her long voyage. Brown also assisted in hiring several masters and mates for the five cutters, and was able to produce the $1,000 Ottinger needed for expenses. There is no mention of towage on the lakes. On October 31, the Captain sailed out of Milwaukee on the 2,325 mile voyage to Boston. His next stop was at Michilimackinac, at the top of the Michigan peninsula, where he was able to pick up the *Isaac Toucey*. She, too, was in winter storage, some 18 miles from her home port. She was hastily rerigged, fitted with furniture and ballast and made ready to sail November 6, under command of one of the masters brought from Milwaukee. The two cutters then proceeded to Detroit on Lake St. Clair for the *Jacob V. Thompson*. Here the Milwaukee men left for home and new masters and mates were hired, along with additional seamen and cooks. Looking ahead to stormy days on the Atlantic, Ottinger ordered five storm sails to be made by Hoffman and McBride of Detroit, and shipped on to Quebec.[11]

The three cutters then went down Lake Erie to Erie for the *Jeremiah S. Black*, and all four went across the lake to Port Colburne on the Canadian shore. Here it was discovered that the *Thompson* had a broken mast. Ottinger telegraphed ahead to his next stop, St. Catherine's, the other side of the Welland

Canal, and a new mast was ready when the fleet arrived. They lost only four hours in having it installed. The trip through the canal, already beginning to freeze up, was hard on some of the cutters. They lost copper sheathing and planking along the way.

Once the mast was installed, Ottinger sent the four cutters under Detroit masters, the length of Lake Ontario to Kingston at the entrance to the St. Lawrence, while he took the train to Oswego to pick up the fifth cutter, *Howell Cobb*. By then most of his men were ready to quit so he hoped to hire replacments at Oswego. He found no one willing to sign on for the whole voyage but, with the help of Customs Collector Charles A. Perkins and his Deputy, William O'Leary, two masters, two mates and two seamen were found. Others signed on and quit at the thought of cold weather ahead.

Ice had already begun to form when he met the four other cutters at Kingston at night in a blinding snowstorm. They cleared Canadian Customs in a hurry, hired a steam tug to pull all five and set off through the canal for Montreal. It was still snowing.

When they reached Montreal all the masters, mates and seamen who had come aboard at Oswego quit and went home. With the help of the American Vice-Consul, I. W. Hawes, enough replacements were found to get the fleet to Quebec.

In wind and snow, they reached the wharves of Quebec's lower town at night December 1. Many of the Masters, mates and seamen, left promptly. Ottinger hastily contacted Commercial Agent A. M. Cohen. He needed supplies, charts, men and repairs. And a steam tug and a pilot had to be found to tow the vessels down the river before it froze.

The storm sails, ordered in Detroit, arrived and were put on board. Enough men were found to provide a master, a mate, a cook and four seamen for each cutter. Agent Cohen produced the necessary charts, and workmen hastened to complete repairs. A tug and a pilot were engaged.[12] All this must have been done at breakneck speed for they were underway the next evening by 8 o'clock. Most of the hired men probably spoke only French, but they were wise in the ways of winter sailing.

Last Down the St. Lawrence

Unfortunately, but understandably, there are no journals or logs to tell of this momentous voyage, but there is an epic letter, written by Captain Ottinger to Secretary Chase when the fleet parted company with the tug and pilot at Green Island River (now Ile Verte) some 120 miles down the St. Lawrence December 3. Headed "On Board U. S. Revenue Cutter *Jeremiah V. Black,* Green Island River, St. Lawrence, December 3, 1861," it reads:

To the Hon. S.P. Chase
Secretary of the Treasury
Sir
    I have the honor to report to You that the Revenue Cutters you directed me to move from the Lakes to the sea coast are now one hundred and twenty miles below Quebec and proceeding seaward.

Delays, by adverse gales and other causes beyond my control, have frequently taken place since I left Milwaukee, at which port prompt dispatch was obtained in getting the cutter fitted for sea, through the attention of E. Brown Esq. Collector of that port.

On arriving at Mackinaw I found the "Isaac Toucey" was laid up in a small river about eighteen miles from that Island. We took on board its equipment, furniture and kentlarge, and the following day brought the "Toucey" into the lake and put ballast and furniture on board, also stores and crew that came in the "Brown" from Milwaukee for that cutter.

At Detroit a master was obtained for the "Jacob Thompson" to go to sea, and one to take the "Toucey" to Erie, Penna. The master who came in charge from Mackinaw did not agree to go any further than Detroit.

I also engaged a master to command one of the cutters from Erie to the sea coast, he having a certificate as ship master issued by the Board of Trade at Liverpool, he proved entirely incompetent however, and left at port Colburne at which place we discovered that the "Thompson's" foremast was broken entirely off at the wedges. I forwarded the dimensions of the several parts of the mast to St. Catherines and made arangements to have a new one made which was completed and put in without delaying the vessels only some four hours.

It was then understood that the cutters were to go to Kingston as soon as practicable and I proceeded to Oswego by railroad at which place there was more difficulty in getting persons to go as masters and mates than I had met with before. The weather was stormy and seamen had been getting such high rates of wages on the lakes that they did not wish for further employment. 3 dollars per day was paid for men by a schr bound westward in the day I arrived at Oswego. After considerable exertion on the part of William O'Leary, Deputy collector, and a shipping master, a crew was obtained who worked on board a few hours and left. Riggers were then employed who agreed to work the "Cobb" to Kingston at 2 dollars per day, and passage back, but in the following day they declined going, and also a person who had agreed to go master to the sea coast informed me he had decided not to encounter the cold weather.

On the third day after arriving at Owego, I succeeded in agreeing with Captain Williams, Captain John Brown, two mates and two seamen to go in the cutters to Boston and in the morning of November 24th we sailed from that port and arrived at Kingston at 6 P.M. in a thick snow storm. On the following day, after attending to business at the Custom House we took steam at 2 P.M. for Montreal, passed through the ice floating in detached fields for about five miles and met another severe snow storm and freezing. On arriving at Montreal the entire party that came on board at Oswego left to go home. I could not obtain any persons suitable for masters, mates or seamen in Montreal and took steam for Quebec, at which port we arrived at night on the 1st of December, blowing strong and snow falling fast.

On the 2nd at 8 P.M. left Quebec in tow of steam tug, with masters and mates for each cutter, one cook and four seamen.

I. W. Hawes Esq. Vice Consul General for the U.S. at Montreal gave me valuable assistance while at that port. A. M. Cohen Esq. U. S. commercial Agent at Quebec gave me important aid in matters of business and in communicating with the Custom House and pilot commissions.

I would further state that it was found necessary to caulk the cutters A. V. Brown, Isaac Toucey & Howell Cobb from the water to the plank sheer and put new pieces in the waterway of A. V. Brown and H. Cobb and several pieces of plank in the deck of each.

For each cutter I had made at Detroit, and forwarded to Quebec, a new foresail for storm sails.

The running rigging of the Howell Cobb had become rotten and new rigging was required throughout.

The two bow anchors were also needed and have been obtained, also charts of the Gulf of St. Lawrence and coast of the U.S. as far as New Bedford. Each cutter has been furnished with some equipment and the lateness of the season has caused an increase of expenditure over the estimate I had the honor of submitting to You. As you did not order the cutters to any particular port, I will endeavor to put them in Boston. We are the last vessels navigating the St. Lawrence. My pilot says that only once before, in thirty years, has any vessel passed down so late.

I am respectfully your humble servant

Douglass Ottinger
Capt U. S. Revenue Marine[13]

Here, at Green Island River, 120 miles below Quebec, they parted with their tow and pilot and the pilot took the Captain's letter to mail. They then bent their sails and headed for the Gulf of St. Lawrence and Cabot Strait. During the voyage of over 1,000 miles through the Strait and outward of Nova Scotia to Boston, the vessels appear to have kept together, but as they neared Boston, the smallest, *Howell Cobb,* fell behind.

The *Brown* reached Boston December 18. The *Black,* with Captain Ottinger on board, came in two days later and the *Thompson* on the 23rd. *Toucey* and *Cobb* were not far behind. It had taken a month to assemble and outfit the fleet on the lakes, and sixteen days for the first cutter to reach Boston from Quebec. The *Brown* had had the longest voyage of all — 2,325 nautical miles from Milwaukee to Boston.

These were momentous days, not only for the five Great Lakes cutters but for Boston as well. Southern diplomats Slidell and Mason, and their entourage, had been captured at sea and had just been brought into Fort Warren as prisoners of war.

Ottinger remained in Boston for a few days with Captain John Whitcomb of the *Morris,* hourly awaiting the arrival of the *Howell Cobb.* He was being entertained Christmas morning in the ward room of the *Morris* when, as the Journal reports, "Suddenly Captain John Whitcomb of this Cutter fell dead upon the floor in the presence of Captain Ottinger and Lieutenant A. A. Fengar."[14]

Nor was this the only tragedy that occurred that Christmas week. On December 29, Lieutenant Fengar received a dispatch from Gloucester saying that the cutter *Cobb* was wrecked near Lane's Cove, Cape Ann. After her long and arduous voyage, the *Cobb* had succumbed in a gale at night on the New England rocks within a few miles of her destination.[15]

The *Morris,* under Fengar, immediately went to her aid. Fengar put into Gloucester, since the weather was bad, and sent men overland to the scene. They rescued the men, but were unable to save the cutter.[16] In the Journal of the *Morris,* it was reported:

> Found her in an ugly position upon the rocks with her bottom and bilges ground to splinters, her stern post out and wood end all open, her forefoot

and from three to four feet of planking completely gone, and cleaned completely out inside, also broken into abaft the waist. The "Howell Cobb is in the hands of the wrecking "Story" and everything is being saved from her that can possible be got off. Made arrangements to take the officers and crew on board.[17]

Ottinger was given a short leave of absence but was soon ordered to command the newly acquired steam cutter *Miami* at New York. Captain Anson L. Hyde was dispatched to Boston to take charge of the four Great Lakes Cutters and repair them for service.[18]

The *Black* was sent to Eastport, Maine, under command of Lieutenant David Moody. At the time of her departure, she was in good condition and was described as a 65 ton schooner, 68 feet long, 16 feet wide, with a depth of 5 feet 8 inches. Her foremast extended 50 feet above deck, her main mast, 54 feet. Topmasts added another 25 feet. The *Black's* sails were good but she needed new rigging.[19]

The *Brown* was later ordered to Salem, Massachusetts, as a guard ship. She was described at that time as a 58-ton schooner, 60 feet long, 17 feet wide and 6 feet deep. She could carry 700 rations and 400 gallons of water. In 1863, she was sent to Beaufort, North Carolina, to police the conquered but troublesome inland waters of that rebel state.[20]

In August 1862, the *Toucey* was ordered to Castine, Maine, under command of the veteran Captain Rufus Coffin. She remained at Castine throughout the war. The *Thompson* remained in Boston until September when she was assigned to the Newport, Rhode Island, station. The *Floyd*, which remained on the Great Lakes, was shifted from Lake Huron to Detroit.[21]

As for the men who had helped Ottinger bring the schooners from Quebec to Boston, Chase wrote Boston Collector Goodrich saying:

Pay Ottinger and tell him to discharge the masters, mates, and crews of the vessels.[22]

In March, when Captain Ottinger took command of the *Miami* at New York, he returned $198.31 to the Treasury Department. It was what he had left out of the $1,000 he had been allowed for expenses.[23]

Strangely, all six of the cutters from the Great Lakes were named for men who seceded from the Union. They kept these names throughout the war.

CHAPTER X

President Lincoln on Board Cutter Miami

President Lincoln spent one of the most eventful weeks of the Civil War on board the Revenue Cutter *Miami* in Chesapeake Bay in May 1862. Was he thinking of this voyage a year later when he wrote James C. Conkling about what to include in a war-time speech to be given at a mass meeting of Union men in Illinois? He told Conkling:

> Nor must Uncle Sam's web-feet be forgotten. At all the watery margins they have been present. Not only on the deep sea, the broad bay and the rapid river, but also up the narrow, muddy bayou, and wherever the ground was a little damp, they have been and made their tracks.[1]

With Captain Ottinger in command, *Miami* was the flagship of the nation from May 5 to 10, 1862. On board were the President, Secretary of the Treasury Salmon P. Chase, Secretary of War Edwin M. Stanton and Brigadier General Egbert L. Viele. Discouraged by the slow progress of the Army and Navy to take Norfolk and advance on Richmond, Lincoln planned his own campaign in the field. The first indication of this came on May 4, when Stanton telegraphed Major General John E. Wool, commanding at Fortress Monroe, saying:

> The President desires to know whether your force is in condition for a sudden movement if one should be ordered under your command. Please have it in readiness.[2]

The *Miami* had been purchased for $25,000 earlier that year in New York from Arthur Leary, a merchant. She was a 115-foot 213-ton screw steamer with two oscillating engines. She had been built on the River Clyde, Scotland, in 1853. Her frame was of English oak; her planking of teak, and her fastenings of copper. As *Lady Le Marchant,* she had been in transatlantic service for six years. When purchased in January 1862, she was completely overhauled and given a new screw and new copper fastenings.[3] One of the ablest men in the Revenue Marine Service, Captain Ottinger, was put in command.

"Call the Steamer the *'Miami'.* Have everything in perfect readiness. Keep her waiting orders until further advised," Chase wrote Collector Barney at New York April 3. It was obvious that *Miami* was destined for important missions. "Provide every particular necessary for comfort," Chase added. "Bed, bedding, crockery, glassware, 2 or 3 spare beds and bedding for use if needed."[4]

A later inventory indicates that the *Miami's* furnishing included ten champagne glasses, a silver coffee urn, two silver tea pots, a silver plated nut-picker and two silver plated snuffers. She was a schooner-rigged steamer carrying ten sails. She had a 24-foot gig, fitted with brass oarlocks and cushions, a 22-foot launch and two cutters (four-oared rowboats).[5]

The *Miami* left New York April 4, 1862 with Barney and Harrington on board, arriving in Washington April 7. She was immediately the object of much attention. On April 9, Secretary Chase took the Secretaries of War and State, together with Admiral Dahlgren and "ladies" down the river to Alexandria and back. More visitors were taken on a short cruise the next day, including Governor Sprague. Two days later Secretary of State Seward, his wife and daughters came on board. Soon after even more important guests arrived. As the Journal reports:

> At 3 P.M. His Excellency 'President' Lincoln, Lady & 2 sons and Lady friends also came on board when we proceeded down the River about one mile below Alexandria and turned to go up to the Navy Yard when we arrived at 5 P.M. and Parties left for the city.[6]

One wonders if Captain Ottinger ever reported to the President that two days after this ceremonial cruise he, as the Journal reports, "thought it prudent to send the quarter master to the Hospital having the small pox."[7]

The President came aboard on more official matters April 19 when he accompanied Chase, Stanton, Dahlgren and other Army and Navy officials down the Potomac to Army headquarters at Aquia Creek. The *Miami's* guns were ready for instant action as she made the voyage. It was at 10 o'clock that night, while the vessel was lying at anchor off headquarters, that the President was informed that General McDowell's troops had captured Fredericksburg. The next day General McDowell himself, with Colonel Bayard and other officers, came on board the *Miami* to be congratulated before she steamed back to the Navy Yard.

The *Miami* was under Army orders but Stanton, Chase and Welles worked closely together, all deferring to the President's wishes in regard to the operation of the cutter. Captain Ottinger remained in command, assisted by Lieutenants Timothy Treadway, W. E. Holloway and A. G. Cary, two engineers and a Revenue Marine Service crew of thirty-four.[8]

By May 2, it was obvious that another mission was in store for the cutter. She was thoroughly scrubbed and special provisions were brought on board, including 30 pounds of coffee, 15 pounds of butter, and 20 pounds of cheese from the Navy yard. She also took on 12 tons of Navy coal. The next day, with the Secretary of War on board, she weighed anchor and proceeded to Aquia Creek where General McDowell came on board. They then returned to Washington, arriving Monday morning May 4.

There was no rest for Ottinger and his men. All hands were mustered at 10 A.M. and the vessel was inspected throughout. The next day she was cleaned, and eight tons of coal were taken on board. The men were paid for the month of April.[9]

Monday, May 5 was a pleasant Spring day, with the wind from the South and Southwest, but by afternoon the wind had shifted into the East and it had begun to rain. By 6 P.M. it was dismal and rainy when, as the Journal reports:

> The President 'Lincoln', Secretary Chase and Secretary Stanton with General Viele came on board 7 P.M. Boat underway and proceeded down the River wind ESE & rain at 8 P.M. Wind and weather the same 8-12 [unintelligible] pleasant but cloudy at 10 P.M. came to anchor a short distance below Mt. Vernon.[10]

Here Pilot Watts of Washington was replaced by Pilot John Rail for the rest of the voyage. Third Lieutenant Cary, keeper of the Journal, ended the day's record with the customary "Ends The Same," noting that 33 rations had been served.

Did Lincoln sleep in the ward room or in the cabin? *Miami* was equipped with a 19-foot cabin containing four beds, and a wardroom containing eight beds. In any event, he had a peaceful anchorage just off the White House, below Mt. Vernon, until 3 A.M. when a brisk northwest wind came up and the *Miami* made sail. She was soon scudding along, under sail alone, at more than ten knots. The top gallant yard and the squaresail were set aloft as she flew down the Potomac and out into Chesapeake Bay. Captain Ottinger and his men rejoiced but below decks some faces, including that of the President, began to turn pale. By lunchtime the President declined to eat and instead stretched out on a locker.[11]

In the afternoon, off Wolf Trap, all hands went to quarters and fired shrapnel from the cutter's two big guns, a 24-pounder and a 12-pounder, and from her pivot gun. The wind died down later and one of the cutter's six awnings was set up on deck for the Presidential party.[12]

Progress was slow later in the day. It was about 9 P.M. before *Miami* tied up alongside the *George Washington* at the wharf at Fortress Monroe. Immediately Secretary Stanton ordered General Wool and his staff aboard the *Miami* for a conference. While the conference was in progress, the cutter cast off "and dropped off into the stream." It was then 1:10 A.M.

In spite of the late hour the President insisted on visiting Commodore Louis M. Goldsborough aboard the *U.S.S. Minnesota*. It is said that a tug carried Lincoln, Stanton, Wool, Chase and Viele to the *Minnesota* in pitch darkness.

The delegation had difficulty in arousing attention. When they were finally heard, they were ordered to the port side (the crew side). Protocol required that Lincoln be the first to ascend the narrow companionway to the deck.[13] No mention is made in the *Miami's* log of the conference or when the tug brought the men back to the cutter but at 5 A.M. they were off to another conference, this one on board the *U.S.S. Vanderbilt*. *Miami* hove up her anchor, steamed close aboard *Vanderbilt* and "sent the President and his party, Secretary Chase and others on board."[14] After conferring, they were rowed back, passing the *USS Monitor* and the cutter *E. A. Stevens*.

Miami then proceeded to Fortress Monroe wharf where General Wool and his staff came aboard. All went ashore for breakfast in Quarters Number One at the Fortress. The *Miami* then went to the lower wharf to take in eight tons of coal.[15]

Lincoln remained on shore all day, first visiting the two ironclads in Hampton Bay, the *Monitor* and the Revenue Cutter *Stevens*, and later traveling on horseback to outlying regions. He spent the night ashore in Quarters Number One.[16]

While taking in coal at the lower wharf, the *Miami* had a slight accident. On an ebb tide she sheared into the wharf. The starboard cathead was carried away. She remained at the wharf all day. At 6 P.M., as the Journal records:

The rebel steamer Merrimac steamed in sight off Sewells Point.[17]

No action developed. It was a stormy night, with northwest winds and rain squalls. Lincoln and Stanton remained ashore but Chase and Viele returned to spend the night on board. Extra lines were brought out to fasten the cutter to the wharf. By 3 A.M. the sea was increasing so the cutter dropped out into the channel for safety. At 6:30 A.M. Captain Ottinger dispatched a boat by orders from Secretary Chase, with a letter to Commodore Goldsborough on *Minnesota*. Later in the day *Miami* was ordered to another wharf where she was made ready for immediate action. Division officers reported their readiness to Captain Ottinger, First Lieutenant Treadway and the other officers. That night, the *Miami* anchored in the harbor, ready for action. Lincoln remained ashore.

Although there is no mention of it in the *Miami's* Journal, the Navy attacked, and silenced, a small battery on the end of Sewell's Point that morning while Lincoln watched. Again the *Merrimack* appeared and disappeared, refusing combat. With Lincoln in command, Army and Navy forces then began searching for the best beach on which to land troops. Obviously it had to be beyond the reach of *Merrimack's* guns.

Early the next morning *Miami* was ordered to the wharf at Fortress Monroe to pick up Secretary Chase and General Wool and his staff. She arrived too early. She cast off and anchored off shore until 8:30 A.M. when Chase and Wool came on board, bringing a pilot to find a beach on which to land the troops. Lincoln, meantime, boarded a tug and, with another pilot, also set out to hunt for a landing. The two vessels searched the shore below Willoughby

Spit in Lynhaven Bay. To reach this shore *Merrimack* would have had to run the gauntlet of Fort Wool and Fortress Monroe.

At 10 A.M. *Miami* "sent both boats on shore at Lynhaven Bay rebel shore to reconnoiter below Willoughby Spit." (This beach is now called "Ocean View.")

Here her men found "three and a half faths of water [21 feet] right into the shore." When the boats returned, the *Miami* herself ran in close to shore (about 500 yards) whereupon a number of people appeared on the shore waving a flag of truce. As the Journal reports:

> Our officers Lieut A. G. Cary in charge of cutter Lieut W. E. Hollaway in charge of Gig with armed boats crew landed to meet them.[18]

The tug on which Lincoln was a passenger was nearby, having approached within 100 yards of the shore. Wool ordered a flag of truce hoisted on *Miami* so a bedsheet was hastily snatched from a bunk and run up on the flag line. Chase may have thought that Norfolk was surrendering for when the boats returned without any passengers, he went ashore himself to talk to the people on the beach. They included one white woman and a number of black persons. They did not want to be taken to Fortress Monroe but were afraid the *Miami* and the tug were going to attack them.

The two vessels then returned to Fortress Monroe. *Miami* anchored off the upper landing until 5 P.M. when the tug carrying Lincoln, Chase and others appeared. Ottinger was then ordered to up anchor and follow the tug "to the rebel coast." This time they reconnoitered a beach which Lincoln favored since it was closer to Norfolk. As the Journal reports:

> On arriving lowered boat with officers and armed men to procede on shore to reconnoiter. On the approach they discovered some men on Horseback—supposed to be Cavalry and returned to the vessel hove up Anchor & proceeded to Fortress Monroe where the Secretary and General Wool and party left.[19]

At 7 P.M. Ottinger received orders to return to Lynhaven Bay and cover with his guns "the landing of our troops on their arrival." Of the two sites reconnoitered it had been decided to use that prefered by General Wool at Ocean View. *Miami* arrived there at 8 P.M. and lowered boats to take soundings. She went as close to shore as possible and dropped her anchor at 9:50 P.M. Then all hands went to quarters. At 1:10 A.M. four troop transports arrived. As the Journal reports:

> Transports landing troops as fast as possible with the assistance of our boats and kedge anchor.[20]

Captain Ottinger went on shore between 4 and 5 A.M. to assist in the landing. At 8 A.M. Secretary Chase and General Wool arrived from Fortress Monroe and went on the beach, after stopping on the *Miami*. Ottinger shifted his lines to let the *Miami* swing in the ebb tide, and it was found that her anchor was unshackled. This was easily mended about 8:30 A.M. Most of her men were on shore assisting the troops who had met no resistance on their landfall.

An hour later, *Miami* ran into trouble. At 9:30 A.M., "a piece of the boiler blew out causing us to blow off steam and put the fires out." *Miami*, with Presidential gear on board, was disabled. Chase heard the bad news when he came on board that morning. He left soon after for Norfolk. The troops took the city easily but the rebels blew up the *Merrimack* before they departed.

Miami was now unable to take the Presidential party back to Washington. The steamer *Baltimore* was engaged for the return voyage. That night, at 11 P.M., she came alongside *Miami*, presumably to pick up the Presidential baggage.[21] The next day, Miami was towed to Fortress Monroe where she waited several days for a boiler maker to make repairs. She returned to Washington May 18, taking with her the safety valve of the *Merrimack* as a present to Lincoln from one of his admirers in Norfolk.[22]

Later in May, *Miami* was ordered to New York where she was anchored off the Battery. In September Captain Ottinger left the cutter to take command of all Revenue Marine activities in North Carolina waters. As the Journal reports:

"At 12:30 P.M. Capt Ottinger left the ship when the rigging was manned and three cheers given."[23]

CHAPTER XI

Cutters on the West Coast

It was thirteen years since the first nugget of gold was found in a mill race near Sacramento; eleven since California achieved statehood; twelve since the Revenue Cutter *Lawrence,* Captain Alexander V. Fraser, had berthed at San Francisco after rounding Cape Horn and sailing almost to Hawaii before entering the Golden Gate. The frenzy of the first gold seekers had subsided. There were still fortunes being made in gold but settlers were finding other charms in the long rugged coast on the Pacific — the climate, the bountiful soil, the Spanish heritage, lumber, fish and whales, and trade with China.

In many parts of California and the territories of Oregon and Washington, might still made right, but in the harbors of San Francisco, Astoria, and Port Townsend, United States Revenue Cutters had brought some order out of maritime chaos. Other cutters had followed the *Lawrence* — the iron bark *Polk,* and the little wooden schooner *Argus* in 1850, the two big wooden schooners *William L. Marcy* and *Jefferson Davis* in 1854 and the *Joseph Lane* in 1855. There to protect the American economy, they also encouraged legitimate trade and, by example, established principles of seamanship, navigation, and humanitarianism learned on the East Coast.

The Civil War was 3,000 miles away by land, 11,000 by sea. The West Coast had little incentive to fight the battles of the East. Slavery was not an issue in California; there were no cotton plantations needing cheap labor; no cotton mills making big profits. The West Coast might well have dropped out of the Union and gone it alone. Instead it sent troop ship after troop ship down the coast to the Isthmus of Panama where soldiers took the new railroad across the narrow neck of land to Aspinwall and boarded ships that headed north to the battlefields. And it sent much needed revenue from its gold ports to finance the costly conflict.

When war was declared, there were three cutters on the West Coast. The *Lawrence* had gone down in the Pacific when, under the command of Captain Ottinger, she struck the beach off San Francisco in 1851.[1] Little *Argus* had been sold in 1853[2] and the *Polk* was auctioned off a year later. She brought $3,350.[3] Remaining were *Marcy, Davis,* and *Joe Lane,* all sailing schooners somewhat the worse for wear.[4]

In 1858, command of the *Marcy* went to Captain William Cooke Pease, one of the first Revenue Cutter men stationed on the West Coast. Pease, a Yankee from Edgartown, Martha's Vineyard, Massachusetts, had navigated the *Polk* around the Horn in 1850, and the *Davis* in 1853-1854, commanded the *Argus* at Benicia in 1850-1853, and the *Davis* in Puget Sound in 1854-1856. He had been the youngest Captain in the service in 1850 at the age of thirty-one. Six years later he superintended the building of the six Great Lakes cutters at Milan, Ohio. He returned to the Pacific to command *Marcy* in 1858.[5]

In April 1861, Pease was ordered by Secretary Chase to fit the *Marcy* at San Francisco for sea "for the purpose of overhauling vessels supposed to be contraband of war, or owned by members of the Confederate states." Rebel vessels and foreign vessels allied with the Confederate cause were already prowling the Pacific sea lanes looking for California vessels loaded with gold.

The *Marcy* was sent up the Bay to Martinez for extensive repairs and new armament. To make sure that she would be easily identified as a defender of the Union, Captain Pease had her eagle figurehead re-gilded and official Revenue Marine insignia painted on gangways and the stern. She was in the shipyard from April until September.[6]

In the meantime, the San Francisco Collector Ira Rankin chartered, at Pease's suggestion, the iron steamer *Santa Cruz* for use as a revenue cutter. As a tribute to Brigadier General Sumner, she was re-named *General Sumner*. She was chartered for $1400 a month, an expense questioned by Secretary Chase. In order to convince him of her worth, Pease sent a letter July 19 to Congressman E. B. Washburne in Washington saying:

"Should you happen at the Treasury Department at anytime within a few days after the receipt of this, may I ask you to impress upon the mind of the Secretary of the Treasury the absolute necessity of approving the course adopted by the Collector here in chartering this vessel (steamer Santa Cruz, now Genl Sumner) for six months at $1400 per month. She is just the vessel we require, and the expense is a mere trifle for a steam cutter to guard the harbor of San Francisco and coast of California.

No dependence can be placed in a sailing vessel here, as none can ever get out of the harbor against a head wind, except with a very strong fair wind, which seldom happens, if ever, at this season of the year.

It behooves us all, even here, to be vigilant and in doing so, we ought to have the means to crush out any attempt on the part of those who would subvert our constitution, with success.

Hoping you may find occasion to further the object the Collector had in view, at an early date."[7]

Chase, Pease, and the Collector need not have worried about the expense of chartering the steam cutter. Her patriotic owner refused payment and donated her services to the Union cause.

Joseph Lane Goes to Mexico

The topsail schooner *Joseph Lane*, originally called the *Campbell*, had been stationed at Astoria, Oregon, for six years when war broke out. Called "Queen of the fleet" for her graceful lines, she was ordered to return to the East Coast in April 1861. She left Astoria in June and sailed to San Francisco where her captain, John S. S. Chaddock, learned that the order had been rescinded. She received armament and in July was ordered to San Diego. Before she left, her men set up a target on Angel Island in San Francisco Bay and spent several days firing at it from the cutter 600 yards off shore. In addition to her regular crew of between 20 and 25, she now had ten "marines" on board.[8]

Orders were changed again. Chaddock was directed by Collector Rankin to by-pass San Diego and go to the Gulf of California with stops at La Paz and Guaymus in Mexican Territory where there were rumors of trouble with Mexican insurgents.

The cutter left San Francisco September 13, reaching La Paz September 28 and Guaymus October 5. Here she was cordially received by the Captain of the port. However, her men were not so cordially received the next morning when they went ashore in the market boat. They found a fierce battle raging between insurgents and government troops. They made a hasty retreat back to the cutter.

Soon after Captain Chaddock saw the flag at half mast on the American consulate. Two officers were immediately dispatched. They returned with Consul Alden who said government troops had ransacked the consulate and tried to put him in prison. They had stolen ten stand of rifles and had seriously wounded Walter Paul, an American. *Joe Lane's* surgeon was sent ashore with bandages. The injured man was brought on board.

Captain Chaddock then moved the cutter closer ashore and anchored her so she swung broadside to the town, where her guns would do the most good if needed. The guns were shotted and aimed but remained silent. All was quiet that night. The next morning First Lieutenant James G. Merryman, sent ashore to investigate, found order restored.

Leaving Guaymus soon after, the cutter returned to La Paz where she spent the next two weeks on a diplomatic mission. While her crew painted and repaired the *Joe Lane*, the officers visited Governor Rivera of Mexico and invited him and his friends to come aboard the cutter. The Governor and several "ladies and gentlemen" were entertained Sunday, October 20, while the crew was given liberty. Salutes were fired and friendly relations established. The occasion was such a success that more residents of La Paz came aboard the following day and more salutes were fired. When the *Joe Lane* left October 24, she was towed out into the Gulf by a Mexican steamer. She reached San Francisco November 14 and discharged the ten "marines."[9]

Franklin Pierce

PRESIDENT OF THE UNITED STATES OF AMERICA,

To all who shall see these presents, Greeting:

Know ye, *That reposing special trust and confidence in the integrity, diligence, and good conduct of William C. Pease I do appoint him Captain of a Cutter in the service of the* United States, *for the protection of the revenue; and do authorize and empower him to execute and fulfil the duties of that office according to law: And to have and to hold the said office, with all the rights and privileges thereunto legally appertaining, unto him, the said William C. Pease during the pleasure of the President of the United States for the time being.*

IN TESTIMONY WHEREOF; *I have caused these letters to be made patent, and the seal of the Treasury Department of the United States to be hereunto affixed.*

GIVEN *under my hand, at the City of Washington, the fifth day of October in the year of our Lord one thousand eight hundred and fifty three and of the Independence of the United States of America the Seventy eighth.*

By the President: *Franklin Pierce*

James Guthrie Secretary of the Treasury

Commission of Captain William Pease

National Archives

11-4

Captain Pease Seizes *NEVA*

While the *Joseph Lane* was in Mexico, Captain Pease was keeping an eye on two suspected vessels, the ship *Ashland* from New Orleans and the 160 ton schooner *Neva*. The *Ashland* was partly owned by her master, Captain Wilson, a Southerner. On October 24, Pease was ordered by Collector Rankin "to keep watch on the *Neva's* movements, she being suspected of being a rebel privateer." When she left the inner harbor and went around to Rincon Point, Pease followed her in *Marcy* and questioned her captain who said she was going to "lay up for the present."

Pease boarded and examined the vessel and found one 12-pounder gun, 12 muskets, four blunderbusses, four pistols, and a dozen swords. *Neva* was then seized and turned over to the military authorities.[10] In Navy records, Pease is credited with capturing a Confederate privateer.[11]

The *Ashland* had been in port since September 30, preparing for a voyage to the Gulf of California where she would collect fertilizer for a San Francisco merchant. Captain Wilson was known to be a rebel. Collector Rankin said later he would have seized the vessel immediately had he been informed of the passage of the law authorizing the seizure of all ships belonging to rebels. Instead he let her slip out of the harbor late in November.

Some weeks later the San Diego Collector notified Rankin that the first mate and several seamen from the *Ashland* had jumped ship south of San Diego and come to him with word of the way captain Wilson had behaved once he dropped his pilot off San Francisco. They claimed he carried on in an "outrageous manner," repudiating his allegiance to the United States and tearing down the flag, swearing it would never again fly over his ship. He stated he would go to Africa and bring slaves back to New Orleans.[12]

The San Diego collector investigated and found that after collecting guano on Georges Island, Wilson went into Guaymus to sign on crew. There he refused to give his papers to the American consul and became abusive, making a "violent, personal, life-threatening attack" on the consul. He unshipped the *Ashland's* rudder, removed her sails, and said he would let her rot before he would hand over his papers. Eventually he was arrested by local authorities and put in jail for 30 days.

Meantime American consuls at both Guaymus and Mazatlan appealed to the San Francisco and San Diego Collectors to seize the *Ashland*. Rankin finally dispatched Acting Lieutenant Scammon of the *Shubrick* with eight men to go to Guaymus by steamer and bring the rebel ship back to San Francisco. When they reached that port, they found that the *Ashland* had been sold to a Mexican while the *U.S.S. Saranac*, Captain Ritchie, stood idly by. Scammon said Ritchie did nothing to stop the sale. He called him "a very feeble and inefficient officer."[13]

Shubrick Replaces Marcy

After commanding the steamer *General Sumner* for several months, Captain Pease did ñot willingly return to the sailing cutter *Marcy* in September although she had been extensively repaired, and at great expense. It was good news to hear in August 1861 that the lighthouse tender, *Shubrick,* a sidewheeler, was to be transferred from the Lighthouse Service to the Revenue Marine Service with himself as commander. On November 13, as noted in the *Shubrick's* journal:

> "Captain Pease with the officers and crew of the Marcy assumed command of the steamer Shubrick. Served 28 rations."[14]

The *Shubrick* had been built at the Philadelphia Navy Yard as a lighthouse tender in 1857. She was made of live and white oak, with copper and iron fastenings. She was 140 feet eight inches long, 24 feet four inches wide, and eight feet deep. She measured 339 tons. She had two masts and could carry a jib, a square sail, a fore Spencer, a topsail, a mainsail and a storm trysail. On deck she carried a 28 foot long gig, modeled after a whale boat, with two masts, two lug sails, and oars. She also carried two small cutters, 27 feet long, and a 17 foot dinghy. They had single masts and sails.

Her armament included two 12-pounder guns, two 12-pounder brass Dahlgren guns, one 24-pounder brass Dahlgren gun, one 30-pounder Rifled Parrott gun, 30 rifles, 51 Colt Navy pistols and holsters, 45 new cutlasses, 30 old cutlasses, and 24 boarding pikes. She could carry 200 barrels of provisions, 1,200 gallons of water, 75 tons of coal, and four cords of wood.[15]

It was to be January 1862, before she was ready for service. *Marcy* was then sent to Puget Sound with Captain Chaddock in command where she came under the jurisdiction of the new and eccentric Customs Collector Victor Smith. Lieutenant Merryman in a report to Secretary Chase in May 1862, indicates that she was later sold in Puget Sound by Collector Smith under questionable circumstances. Other records indicate she was transferred to the Coast Survey.

On March 5, 1862, Chase had telegraphed Collector Rankin at San Francisco saying:

> Turn over the cutter *Marcy* to Commander Sands of the Navy for Coast Survey purposes as per letter by mail[16]

The Shubrick in San Francisco

On January 13, the *Shubrick's* fires were started and she commenced to get up steam. Her first mission was to seek two vessels in distress said to have gone ashore off San Francisco in Half Moon Bay. She found only one of them, the Dutch schooner, *Alpha,* Captain Cooper, wrecked on the shore near Spanish Town, her 9,000 pounds of sugar scattered on the sand. Captain Pease rescued the crew and one lady passenger.[17]

Five days later the steamer was ordered "to get underway for the purpose of going up the Sacramento River to relieve the Depressed Rancheries from the Flood." Heavy rains had caused the river to overflow and many were homeless. Picking up supplies furnished by San Francisco Relief, Captain Pease steamed through Carquinez Straits to the river. At Georgiana Slough he rescued 27 men, women, and children, took them on board, and gave them food and clothing. After transferring them to the *Antelope*, which was returning to San Francisco, he picked up 22 more and put them aboard the steamer *Chrisopoles*. Before he returned to San Francisco he had rescued another 18.[18]

Soon after the rescue, the Captain went aboard the ship *Vitula* to quell a mutiny. Nineteen members of the crew were put in irons and taken ashore to jail. He also assisted the *Flying Dragon* aground on Island Rock near Little Angel. On February 8 the cutter towed the sailing cutter *Joseph Lane* (en route to Puget Sound) out to sea, and on the following day was back in port to assist the U.S. Army. As reported in the Journal February 15, 1862:

> At 10 A.M. Joint Committee on military affairs appointed by the State Senate to inspect the various land points and sights of the Harbour, in view to fortify such places that might be necessary agreeable to the recommendations of the Secretary of War.[19]

On board were "General Wright and his staff, Colonel de Russey and staff of the Army, Collector Ira J. Rankin and company." The *Shubrick* took the men to Fort Alcatrez in the morning, and later sailed them past Larrie Point, Point Bonita, Mile Rock, Fort Point, Raccoon Straits, Waterman Stone Quarry, and Mission Rock. Two days later the telegraph brought word of the Union victory at Fort Donelson and the surrender of 15,000 Confederate soldiers. Captain Pease "dressed ship with colors in honor of this achievement."

On February 26 he assisted the steamer *Nevada,* her bow high and dry on the beach near Rio Vista, and on March 15, took Captain Stanley, a United States lighthouse inspector and his assistants out to inspect the Farallones Lighthouse. They brought the assistant light keeper, William Underwood, ashore April 3. On April 29, the *Shubrick* towed the clipper ship *Sierra Nevada* off Fort Point.

On a constant lookout for enemy ships, the *Shubrick* patrolled off shore in May and June. On May 4 she spoke the clipper ship *Mary T. Robertson,* 125 days from New York, bound to China. The same day, the 24-pounder Howitzer was exercised with several rounds of shrapnel. She spoke the barks *Charles Devans, Nahumkeag,* and *Sunshine* on May 31 and assisted the steamer *Orizaba.* When in the harbor, she frequently anchored off Meiggs Wharf.[20]

Some commercial interests did not appreciate all the rescue work *Shubrick* did. When she pulled the steamer *Nevada* off the beach in the vicinity of the Sacramento River, six steamboat towing companies protested her action to Secretary of the Treasury Chase, claiming the *Nevada* had struck in inland waters 65 miles from San Francisco. They said the *Shubrick* was "interfering with the legitimate rights of Citizens owning steamers adapted to and employed in the towing business."[21]

Chase wrote to San Francisco Collector Rankin reminding him of the Act of Congress of December 22, 1837 which authorized cutters to cruise along the coast in severe weather and to render aid to distressed navigators, but said he did not believe this meant they were to make a practice of towing vessels. Only vessels in distress, or where there was danger to life or property, could claim assistance. Steamers on inland waters should in general look to private parties or companies when in trouble.

"It is my purpose," he wrote, "to keep them [Revenue Cutters] actively cruising, and ready at all times to render the most efficient aid to the Revenue, and as far as it can be done, to the Commerce of the country."[22]

Early in the war, after a conference with Secretary Welles and other Navy men, Lincoln had reported:

> then and there with their unanimous concurrence I directed that an armed revenue cutter should proceed to sea to afford protection to the commercial marine, and especially the California treasure — ships on their way to this coast.[23]

There is no evidence that *Shubrick* ever patrolled beyond the three-mile limit or encountered a privateer. Although *Shenandoah* and other armed rebel vessels prowled the Pacific on the hunt for cargoes of gold, they kept well off shore, far beyond the range of California's one steam cutter.

Chinese immigration, a problem since the early 1850's, continued to keep Pease on the alert for illegally overcrowded vessels from the Orient.

A Troublemaker in Puget Sound

When the *Shubrick* towed the *Joe Lane* out to sea February 8, 1862, the *Joe Lane* did not return to her former station at Astoria, Oregon, but sailed to Puget Sound where Secretary Chase's new appointee and friend, Collector Victor Smith, was keeping not only the Custom House but much of Washington Territory in a state of confusion. Zealous to raise funds for the Treasury Department, he had the mail delivered by Revenue Cutter, turned the cutter *Davis* into a hospital ship, gave the Custom House funds to a friend for safe-keeping, allegedly sold the *Marcy*, and aimed to move the Custom House from Port Townsend, where it had been located since Washington attained territorial status, to Port Angeles. If anyone disagreed with him, he immediately suspected that person of being in league with the Confederacy.

A former newspaper man from Cincinnati, Ohio, Smith knew little about Customs, or the Pacific Coast, or Revenue Cutters, but proceeded to make drastic changes in policies not only in Washington Territory but in California and Oregon as well. By the Spring of 1862, he had made so many enemies that he was obliged to return East to seek support in Washington, and to persuade Congress to change the location of the Custom House. He left Lieutenant Merryman of the *Joe Lane* in charge of Customs at Port Townsend while he was away.[24]

Returning via San Francisco in the summer, Smith commandeered the *Shubrick,* saying she was needed in Puget Sound. Captain Pease, either ill or pretending to be ill, turned command of the cutter over to Lieutenant John Wilson. They reached Port Townsend August 1, 1862, where Merryman was in charge of the Custom House.

Merryman, aghast at Smith's records and actions, and unwilling to believe that Secretary Chase had not fired him, refused to let him into the Custom House whereupon Smith ordered Lieutenant Wilson to train the guns of *Shubrick* on the town. There were some tense moments before Smith managed to get the money and the records from Merryman and sail away to the site of the new Custom House.

Pease returned to the command of the *Shubrick* in Puget Sound in August and spent several unhappy months doing the bidding of the odd Collector, who was in constant fear that the *Shubrick* and the *Joe Lane* would be seized by Canadians in league with Confederates. By then a grand jury at Olympia had indicted Smith on charges of embezzlement, issuing false vouchers and resisting a public officer, but he continued his strange operations. On December 3, he abruptly removed Pease from command of the *Shubrick* and put him ashore at Victoria, Vancouver, saying that a plot existed to turn the *Shubrick* into a Confederate privateer. He hinted that Pease was a Southerner.[25]

Meantime, in the East, President Lincoln and Secretary Chase argued over Smith's strange actions. Lincoln wanted him removed from office, which hurt Chase's feelings. Finally Lincoln took the bull by the horns. When Chase was away May 8, 1863, he wrote him a letter saying, in part:

"My mind is made up to remove Victor Smith as Collector of Customs at Puget Sound."[26]

It was too late to do Captain Pease and Lieutenant Merryman any good. They had been ordered East by the San Francisco Collector at Smith's insistence. To assuage Chase, who was infuriated by Smith's dismissal and threatened to resign as Treasury Secretary, Lincoln allowed Smith to be appointed Superintendent of Lights in Puget Sound. He continued in that capacity until both he and Captain Chaddock were drowned in the wreck of the *Brother Jonathan* off Crescent City, California July 30, 1865.[27]

Pease and Merryman were both acquitted of any complicity in the rebel cause. Pease was sent to Newport to command the *Jacob Thompson*, one of the cutters he had helped to build for the Great Lakes. Merryman was ordered to Portland, Maine to take command of the ill-fated *Caleb Cushing*. Both men later played important parts in convoying the Cotton Fleet from Savannah to New York in 1865 and in re-establishing the Revenue Cutter Service in the South after the war. Merryman remained in the service until 1870. Pease died of typhoid fever aboard the cutter *Kewanee* in Charleston on December 30, 1865.[28]

Four of the leading Revenue Marine officers on the West Coast — Pease, Merryman, Wilson and Chaddock — were recalled to the east in the Spring of 1863. Command of the *Shubrick* went to Captain Charles M. Scammon, and of *Joe Lane* to Lieutenant James M. Selden. These were the only two cutters on the Pacific at that time.

CHAPTER XII

Cushing Captured at Portland, Maine

Two fishermen, Eldridge Titcomb and Albert P. Bibber, were setting a trawl about eight miles southeast of Damariscove Island, Maine, Friday morning the 26th of June 1863. Bibber later said he owned the small boat they were in, but Titcomb claimed they owned it in common, and trawled in common.[1]

"Pretty near the end of the trawl," as Titcomb said, "a schooner run down and spoke to us and ordered us to go alongside." They declined, saying that they were "underrunning" the trawl, and could not be interrupted. They ignored the schooner and went on working.[2]

Some of the men on the schooner then lowered a boat and rowed over to them. Looking up from the trawl, Titcomb saw they had pistols and knives in their belts although they looked like ordinary seamen. They persisted in their invitation. Soon the two fishermen saw there was no use resisting them so they "slipped off the trawl" and rowed to the schooner. Their boat was taken in tow and they went on deck. One of the men told them that they were from the Confederate steamer *Florida*. Titcomb and Bibber didn't know anything about the *Florida*. If they had, they would have realized they were in for trouble. The *Florida* had run the blockade at Mobile with Captain James Newland Maffitt at the helm, and had plundered shipping on the South Atlantic. The schooner was not the *Florida* but these men had been in her crew. When the *Florida* seized the schooner *Clarence* off the coast of Brazil, Maffitt turned the seized vessel over to some of his men with Captain Charles W. (Savvy) Read as commander. Savvy, a 23-year-old graduate of the Naval Academy at Annapolis, had joined Maffitt after fighting in the battle for New Orleans. He was a real daredevil. Proceeding up the coast he captured the *Tacony, M. A. Shindler* and *Kate Stewart,* sending the latter to Philadelphia as a cartel with the *Shindler's* passengers. He transferred to the *Tacony* and destroyed the *Clarence*. He then burned or bonded 19 vessels before the Navy ordered a dozen vessels to be chartered and manned to search for him.[3]

On June 24, Savvy took the fishing vessel *Archer* of Southport, Maine, and shifted his crew to the new prize to elude the Union vessels chasing him. He then burned the *Tacony*.

Titcomb and Bibber had no idea that the schooner they boarded was privateering, or that the young man in the dark pants and frock coat who commanded her was Savvy the "pirate." In fact, it seemed to them that all this was just a prank of fishermen "who had just been fitted out from Portland and had been drinking and wanted to have a spree with us."[4]

They soon learned otherwise. As they sailed westward, the young captain asked many questions about Portland—what time the steamers came and went, how many forts there were, the best passages, and if there was a cutter in the harbor. The fishermen gave evasive answers. Bibber said he thought he saw the cutter going into Boothbay. Asked to pilot *Archer* into Portland, they declined, saying that they did not know how to pilot a deep-draft vessel like the schooner. As they sailed across Casco Bay, the fishermen saw arms being brought up from below. After sunset they entered the harbor and anchored about a third of a mile off Pomeroy Rock. About nine o'clock that night they were sent below and told to stay there or suffer serious consequences. They crawled into the berths assigned to them but could not sleep a wink. Until midnight there was much commotion on deck. After that all they could hear was the tramp of the watchman's feet. At daybreak they were told to come up and get into their boat. It was still not quite light, and there was no wind.

It was hard to believe what they saw. A few hundred yards away, the cutter *Caleb Cushing*, with all her sails set, was being silently towed out of the harbor by two boats.

Both men were rowed to the cutter but Titcomb was sent back to the *Archer* to help get her underway.[5]

The Rebels Invade Portland Harbor

Thwarted in his hopes of entering Hampton Roads, Savvy had decided to invade Portland Harbor and seize one of the two large steamers, *Forest City* and *Chesapeake*, which sailed between Portland and New York, or, failing that, take the revenue cutter. His dreams also included bombarding Portland and planting the Confederate flag on Maine territory.

As he entered Portland Harbor, the *Chesapeake* was docked at the Franklin Wharf, the *Caleb Cushing* was at anchor and small sailboats darted around off Cushing Island where a dance was in progress at the big old wooden Ottawa House. Forts Preble and Lincoln loomed in the distance. A June moon hung in the sky, and Savvy knew he would have to wait until it set after midnight to carry out his daring plan. So he waited patiently as music from the Ottawa House dance drifted over the harbor.

The one engineer in his crew said it would be impossible for him to handle as large a steamer as the *Chesapeake*. Savvy was then obliged to settle for the cutter. He had some idea he might intercept and destroy the *Forest City* which was due to arrive about 4 A.M.[6]

Savvy did not know that *Caleb Cushing* was ready to go in search of his former command *Tacony* whose ashes now lay at the bottom of the sea off Southport. On July 24 Portland's Custom Collector Jedidiah Jewett had wired Secretary of the Treasury Chase saying:

> The underwriters here have requested me to send the Caleb Cushing out to cruise for pirate Tacony. Shall I provide and dispatch her immediately under command of the 1st Lieut.[7]

Jewett was told by Chase to load the cutter with ammunition but to delay her departure until Lieutenant James Merryman arrived to command her. He was due to reach Portland on the *Forest City* early July 27 to replace Captain George Clarke who was terminally ill. In fact Captain Clarke died July 26 and many of *Cushing's* men were ashore that day and night laying him out and arranging his funeral. About half the crew was on board the cutter under the command of Lieutenant David Davenport, a native of Georgia, faithful to the Union although he had once been accused by a disgruntled junior officer of favoring the Confederacy. He had failed his examinations several times but had been allowed to remain on board *Cushing*.

As Lieutenant Davenport lay asleep in his cabin after moonset July 27, Savvy and his men rowed across the harbor with muffled oars and clambered aboard the cutter, scuffled with the one watchman on deck (the other had gone below) and hoisted the sails. Davenport came on deck in his night clothes and was handcuffed. With a total lack of wind the sails hung lifeless so Savvy ordered two boats lowered to tow her out of the harbor. At least the tide was in his favor. It is alleged that Savvy then went into the cabin and donned the late Captain Clarke's uniform, several sizes too big for him.[8]

After taking Bibber on board and ordering the *Archer* to follow the cutter. Savvy stole out of the harbor passing, at close quarters, the steamer *Forest City* coming in with Lieutenant Merryman on board. The steamer's baggage master, Reuben Clark, who was later to reminisce about the episode, saw the cutter leaving under tow but thought nothing of it. Some reports say that Merryman also saw the departing cutter.

Once out of the harbor and past Fort Preble, Savvy hoisted sail and went below to have a gam with Lieutenant Davenport whom he chided for not joining the Confederacy. *Archer* limped behind. Both Bibber and Titcomb were asking to be put ashore and both were promised they would be given their freedom before dark.[9]

Portland in a Frenzy

In Portland, *Cushing's* boatswain stumbled down to the wharf, somewhat the worse for wear after a night ashore. He looked out in the harbor and could not see the cutter. Then as the *Forest City's* baggage master said later:

Well! The cat jumped out of the bag and all Hell broke loose![10]

It was immediately thought that Georgia-born Lieutenant Davenport had made off with the cutter. Aroused from his sleep Customs Collector Jewett sent a telegram off to Secretary Chase saying that the cutter was gone and that "Lt. Davenport in command did not report before sailing."[11]

On the waterfront an angry mob heaped cries of "traitor" on the hapless Davenport, waving pitchforks and muskets as they sought to organize an expedition to recover the cutter. Mayor Jacob McClellan commandeered the *Forest City*, the *Chesapeake* and a tug to go in pursuit. Bales of cotton were brought on board to protect the steamers' paddle wheels. Collector Jewett called up two dozen men from the 7th Maine Volunteers who arrived, breathless, with their regimental band. The steamers were stocked with provisions for a long expedition, and, with the band playing, crowds of citizens tried to get aboard. The Mayor allowed about 50 armed men to cross the gangplank of each vessel and turned the hose on the rest of them. He boarded the *Chesapeake*. Lieutenant Merryman managed to remain on board the *Forest City*.[12]

As the steamers left the harbor, women stood on the rocks waving flags and handkerchiefs and urging the men on to victory. Off Fort Preble the steamers were joined by two tugs with guns and 100 men from the 7th Maine Regulars.[13]

Meantime, 12 miles out, there was little wind and the *Cushing* dawdled along. Savvy, in his oversized uniform, offered Davenport a cigar and removed his handcuffs. From Davenport he learned that the cutter had been prepared to search for the *Tacony* and was loaded with ammunition but the key to the magazine was missing. When the cutter was seized Davenport had thrown it overboard! There was only a small amount of ammunition available.

Some miles behind the *Cushing*, the *Archer* plodded along. Titcomb was still begging to go ashore in his boat which was being towed behind. The three rebels on board were highly elated with their escapade, and Titcomb had to agree that it was "a very daring act." They could not see the *Cushing* but about ten miles out they spotted a steamer between Halfway Rock and Outer Green Island.

On the cutter, Bibber was also asking to go ashore. The answer was "no." Savvy said they were going to stand off a little farther and then heave to and wait for the *Archer* to "come up." She was not yet in sight. They were just past Cod Ledge when a steamer appeared about two miles away. Bibber again asked to leave. The Captain said then he "didn't care" and that the fisherman might take either of the little boats that were alongside. Bibber wasted no time in climbing into a boat and rowing away. From the deck of the cutter a man called to him to "do a little quartering," saying they were going to fire on the steamer. Bibber reached the steamer, the *Forest City*, safely and went on board to tell his strange story.[14]

Meantime, Savvy Read fired what ammunition he had at the *Forest City*, and then seeing two other vessels approach, knew that his luck had run out.

He ordered the cutter's men on deck and told them to get in a boat and row away. Lieutenant Davenport's irons had been removed but the others, except the cook, still wore manacles. As they were rowing away, one of the rebels threw them the keys. By then, with both *Forest City* and *Chesapeake* approaching, Savvy was getting ready to set the cutter on fire and abandon her. Davenport and his men rowed to the *Chesapeake* and climbed aboard.

Bibber was the first to arrive at the *Forest City*. Next came Captain Read and his crew. Soon after, there was a tremendous explosion and the cutter almost immediately disappeared. In what must have been a dramatic moment on board *Forest City*, the young rebel surrendered his sword to Captain Merryman. The steamer then proceeded to take the *Archer* in tow, and all headed back to Portland.[15]

Telegrams to Secretary Chase

The telegraph office at Portland was kept busy that day. When Collector Jewett, waiting anxiously on shore, heard that the *Cushing* had exploded, he immediately sent the following telegram to Secretary Chase:

"Lieutenant Davenport while other Lieutenants were on shore ran off with the cutter Caleb Cushing last night. Soon as advised this morning I put field pieces on Boston and New York steamers and a tug. Sent detachment from 17th regulars and Maine seventh on steamers. They overhauled her ten miles off. She fired on them several rounds but finding that she would be captured they abandonned and then set fire to her and she blew up. The steamers have not returned to report what became of the crew. Her best men were on shore on leave — new commander arrived this morning and went off in a steamer."[16]

As soon as the *Forest City* reached shore, Merryman hastened to the telegraph office and also wired Chase. He said:

"Arrived here this morning at four o'clock was on board the steamer Forest City saw cutter blown up. Lieut Reid of rebel navy was in command & surrendered his sword to me. Twenty-eight prisoners."[17]

In another telegram, the Collector said there were 22 prisoners. He wired:

"Twenty-two men from a confederate vessel entered our harbor last night in the prize schooner Archer boarded the cutter overpowered her crew and made sail in her. They came to burn the gun boats here. We have captured their vessel and all of them and have landed them at Fort Preble. No one injured by cutter's shot. She sank immediately after she blew up.[18]

In still another telegram from C. F. Sanford, Chase was told:

"The Confederate pirates came to this port in Schr. Archer of Southport recently captured and was recaptured by our steamers and towed to the port by Forest City. The crew of the cutter has just marched to station house under guard of a detachment of troops from 7th Maine and 17th Regulars. Confederate pirates have gone to Ft. Preble in irons."[19]

The American Telegraph Company.

PRINTING AND MORSE LINES.

DIRECT TO ALL STATIONS IN THE UNITED STATES AND BRITISH PROVINCES.

OFFICES.—432 Pennsylvania Av?, U. S. CAPITOL, and Willard's
and Metropolitan Hotels, Washington, D. C.

TERMS AND CONDITIONS ON WHICH THIS AND ALL MESSAGES ARE RECEIVED BY THIS COMPANY FOR TRANSMISSION.

In order to guard against errors or delays in the transmission or delivery of messages, every message of importance ought to be REPEATED by being sent back from the station at which it is to be received, to the station from which it is originally sent. Half the usual price for transmission will be charged for repeating the message, and while this Company will, as heretofore use every precaution to ensure correctness, it will not be responsible for errors or delays in the transmission or delivery a repeated messages beyond FIFTY dollars, unless a special agreement for insurance be made and paid for at the time of sending the message, and the amount of risk specified on this agreement: nor is the Company to be responsible for any error or delay in the transmission or delivery of any unrepeated message, BEYOND FIVE DOLLARS, unless in like manner specially insured and amount of risk paid for at the time. No liability for any error or neglect by any other Company over whose lines this message may be sent to reach its destination. No liability for any errors in cipher messages.

CAMBRIDGE LIVINGSTON, Sec'y,   E. S. SANFORD, Pres't.
145 BROADWAY, N. Y.

COMPLAINTS SHOULD BE SENT TO THE SECRETARY.

3N Dated _Portland_ _9 / th_ 1863.

Rec'd, Washington, _June 27_ 1863, _ _ o'clock, _ _ min. M.

To Hon S. P. Chase

Arrived here this morning at four oclock was on board the steamer Forest City saw cutter blown up Lieut Read of rebel navy was in command & surrendered his sword to me — Twenty eight prisoners,

J. H. Merriman

35 / 38.5

Telegram reporting the destruction of the cutter _Caleb Cushing_

Bibber and Titcomb, taken to Fort Preble with the rebels, were released after extensive questioning. Davenport was sent to the cutter *Toucey* at Castine, Maine, and Captain Merryman was ordered to the *Campbell* at New London. The Collector continued to believe that the rebels had come to Portland to seize the two new Navy gunboats, the *Agawam* and the *Pontoosac,* which had been built in Portland and were floating at the Franklin Wharf, but apparently Savvy Read knew nothing about them. Titcomb and Bibber testified that there had been no mention of them during their conversations with him.

The prisoners were marched through flag-waving mobs to Fort Preble where they became the tourist attraction of the day. They made front page news until the Battle of Gettysburg a week later.

Savvy and his crew were taken from Portland, silently and at night, to spend 16 months of confinement in Fort Warren in Boston Harbor. They left with only the clothes they wore, the rest of their possessions having been distributed as relics to the people of Portland. Exchanged in late 1864, Read was given command of another rebel vessel. When Lee surrendered, he burned her and went over the side. He continued to plague the Revenue Cutter Service after the war when he engaged in smuggling, and ran gunboats to both sides in a civil war in Colombia. Eventually he settled down, to some extent, as harbor master in New Orleans.[20]

Dobbin Replaces Cushing

The *Dobbin* was sent to Portland from her station on the Delaware to replace *Cushing.* She had a curious reception at the Maine port when she arrived under command of Captain Webster August 13, 1863. As she sailed into the harbor with her Revenue flags at the peak and her cutter number on the mast head, a gun was fired at her from Fort Preble. It was a blank charge, but it was followed by another shot with a cannon ball that splashed into the water near her. Captain Webster immediately hove to, lowered a boat and sent Lieutenant John A. Henriques ashore to explain that they were friend not foe. Officers at the fort said that no one had told them that the cutter was coming. After the *Cushing* episode, they were understandably cautious.[21]

The *Dobbin* remained in Portland until January 1865. During most of her stay, she cruised in search of privateers and boarded about 50 vessels a day. Webster paid particular attention to Maine's fishermen who were inclined to ignore or misinterpret the fishing laws. A boat with a codfish license was found to have a try works on board, the owner explaining that he aimed to try out "pogies." Webster was stern with the law-breaking fishermen. He threatened to turn the guns on one of them and sink his boat if he refused to obey revenue rules.

Late in August the *Dobbin* was sent to find two of Savvy Read's men who had escaped from Fort Warren in Boston. Webster found them on a schooner off Cape Porpoise and brought them and their boat back to Portland. Later that year he was ordered to leave the *Dobbin* in Portland and go aboard the *U.S.S. Agawam* with his lieutenant and 24 men to search for the steamer

Chesapeake which had been captured by the rebels. Meantime 38 men from the U.S. gunboat *Acadia* and a detachment of soldiers were put on the *Dobbin* to guard her in his absence. The *Chesapeake* was found in Nova Scotia by another vessel. Webster and his men were back in Portland within a week.[22]

The following March, *Miami* was ordered from New York under command of Lieut. Alvin H. Fengar to Halifax and St. John's to bring back the *Chesapeake* and the rebels who had seized her. Stopping at Portland on the way down east, she, like *Dobbin*, was greeted with gunfire from Fort Preble by mistake. At Portland, Fengar learned that another vessel had taken the rebel prisoners on board but that he was to convoy the *Chesapeake* from St. John's to New York. At St. John's he armed the *Chesapeake* with rockets, blue lights, swords and pistols and put one of his lieutenants in command. They both ran into a snow squall and barely made it to Portland. Fengar left *Miami* at Portland for repairs, among them some new wings for her eagle figurehead.[23]

Miami, called "a poor little outcast," was sent out again in August 1864 to chase the privateer *Tallahassee* which had burned 15 vessels in Atlantic. Fengar despaired of catching her, saying:

> Oh for a well armed steamer of eight hundred or a thousand tons now under my feet. I think I could catch her. I will do the best I can with the little Miami however if I have the opportunity.[24]

The Wreck of the *Bohemia*

In 1863 and 1864 there were many mutinies and wrecks off the coast of Maine. The most notable was the wreck of the British mail steamer *Bohemia* which went ashore on the rocks near Cape Elizabeth the night of February 23, 1864, in a snowstorm. Her passengers and crew were rescued before Webster's men reached her the next day. They found her sunk, with the sea making a complete break over her. She carried valuable cargo and was immediately overrun with plunderers. Some of the *Dobbin's* men were detailed to stand guard and protect any property that washed ashore. They had to fire on some of the plunderers to drive them off. Several were taken in custody. It was June before the Collector recalled the men from the wreck, saying there was now "no necessity" for them to look after it.[25]

Under command of Captain Usher after June 1864, the *Dobbin* continued to cruise in search of rebel privateers. In October each man on the cutter received $100 for war duty from the State of Maine. In January 1865 *Dobbin* left Portland to be stationed at Edgartown on Martha's Vineyard, Massachusetts.[26]

CHAPTER XIII

Sail Bows to Steam

By 1865 steam cutters in the Revenue Marine outnumbered sailing cutters twenty to thirteen. In the last years of the war only one sailing cutter was added to the fleet. She was the small *Antietam* purchased in Baltimore as the guard ship for New Bern, North Carolina, in 1864. Eleven of the 1860 sailing cutters and two of those acquired from the Coast survey were still afloat and useful. Two (the *Marcy* and the *Davis*) were decommissioned in 1862 and the *Cushing* was blown up in 1863. The yachts *Henrietta* and *Hope* had seen short service[1] as had the schooner *Joe Miller* and the sloop *Cruiser*.[2]

Four sailing cutters were decommissioned the year the war ended. The *Jackson*, after 33 years in service, and the *Forward*, after 23 years, were sold at Baltimore. The *Allen* is not listed after November 1865, and the *Varina* was returned to the Coast Survey about the same time.

Joe Lane, Morris, Toucey, Black and *Crawford* were decommissioned in the late 1860's: the *Joe Lane* at Port Townsend, Oregon; *Morris* at Baltimore; *Black* at Philadelphia; *Toucey* at New Haven and *Crawford* at Newport. In the 1870's the *James Campbell* was sold in New York for $3,855 and the *Thompson* at Baltimore for $1,400.[3]

The *Dobbin* remained in service until 1881, becoming the first school ship of the Revenue Cutter Service in 1877, taking cadets on practice cruises out of Curtis Bay, Baltimore. She was sold at Baltimore in 1881 for $5,166. She had cost $9,000 when built at J. M. Hood's yard in 1853.[4]

The service's first successful steam cutter, the *Harriet Lane*, after being sold to the Navy was captured by the rebels in 1863. The three steam tugs, *Reliance, Tiger* and *Hercules*, were used mainly on Chesapeake Bay. In 1861 the steamer *General Sumner* was chartered for San Francisco until the steamer *Shubrick* was transferred from the Lighthouse Service to the Revenue Marine Service.

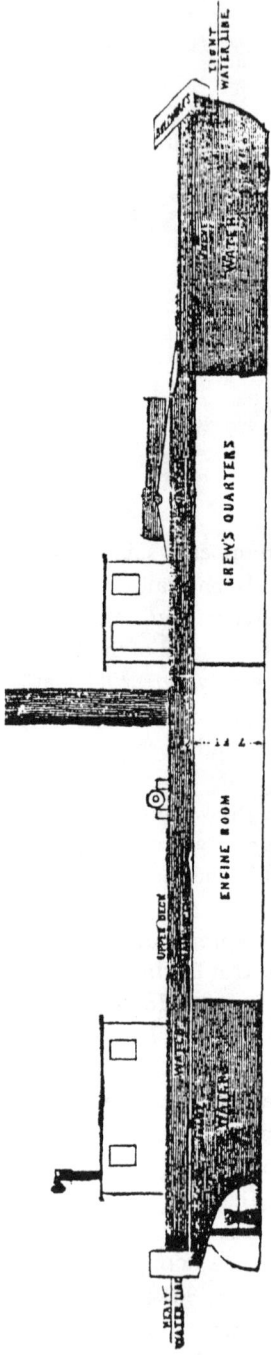

LONGITUDINAL SECTION OF THE "NAUGATUCK"

THE STEVENS IRON STEAM GUNBOAT "NAUGATUCK," NOW AT FORTRESS MONROE

Harper's Weekly

Ironclad *E.A. Stevens (Naugatuck)*

In 1862 three more steamships were acquired - the *Miami* (described in Chapter 10) on which President Lincoln took his historic cruise, the *Flora*, later called *Nemaha*, and the *E. A. Stevens*.

The *Flora-Nemaha*

Flora was 281-ton steam vessel built in Brooklyn and registered for coastwise trade April 17, 1854.[6] She was purchased in New York in 1862 by the Revenue Marine for Army use at Port Royal, South Carolina, by Collector Barney with Revenue Marine Funds for $18,000 and put in commission and armed for an additional $8,422.62. Under command of Lieutenant Rufus Coffin, she was sent to Port Royal in March 1862 to assist in operations against rebel forces in South Carolina and Georgia. Coffin was soon relieved by Lieutenant Alvan A. Fengar. In July the Army took over the cutter, dismissing Fengar and his officers. Engineers and crew were given the opportunity to remain aboard but most of them declined because Army wages were lower than those in the Revenue Marine. In 1864, the *Flora* was renamed *Nemaha*, repaired at a cost of about $31,000, returned to Port Royal, and again staffed by Revenue Marine men. She remained at Port Royal until war's end,[7] her expenses payable out of the cotton fund with money derived from the sale of confiscated cotton.

The Hoboken Ironclad *E. A. Stevens* (Naugatuck)

One of the most unusual cutters in the fleet was the semi-submersible *E. A. Stevens*, sometimes erroneously called the *Naugatuck*. She was the invention of Edwin Augustus Stevens, born in 1795 and well known by 1860 as an engineer, inventor and financier. His home in Hoboken, overlooking the North River and Manhattan, became the Stevens Institute of Technology. On the riverfront below, he built the twin-screw ironclad steamer that was to play a part in the Monitor- Merrimack encounter at Hampton Roads in May 1862. His brother, John, with whom he worked, designed and sailed the schooner *America* which brought America's Cup to the United States in 1851.[8]

The cutter was originally named *Naugatuck* by Stevens himself, but when it was suggested that she be christened "*E. A. Stevens*," he was highly gratified. The cutter bore two names throughout her lengthy existence. Stevens had been working for 20 years on an ironclad for the Navy which was never finished or launched. In 1861 he began construction of the 101 foot semi-submersible ironclad, with two propelling engines, which could take on board enough water, in fore and aft compartments, to sink her almost three feet in 15 minutes. The ballast could be pumped out in half that time. She was a shoal draft vessel, drawing only four and a half feet when without ballast. She had white cedar bulwarks and was designed to carry one 100-pounder rifled gun, and two 12-pounder howitzers forward in a bow opening. The muzzles of the guns could be lowered beneath the deck and the guns loaded from below. She could carry provisions for 60 days.[9]

Stevens offered her to the government in 1861 at no expense. When she was nearing completion late that year, Captain Faunce was detailed to work with Stevens in outfitting and arming her. A gun from the West Point Foundry, superintended by Captain R. R. Parrott, was ordered for her by the Secretary of War but the Navy refused to supply two 12-pounders. These were subsequently purchased by Collector Barney. Also requisitioned were 12 muskets, 12 pistols, and 12 cutlasses. In addition to Revenue Cutter officers, her crew would consist of a coast pilot, a boatswain, a gunner, two quartermasters, ten seamen, two boys, a ship's cook, a steward, two engineers, and two firemen.[10]

Secretary Chase was eager to get her to Norfolk as soon as she was finished. On March 12, 1862, he wrote Barney saying:

> "I hope the vessel will be able to leave New York Saturday. Hasten her to Norfolk."[11]

One of Stevens' men, W. W. Shippen, was made temporary captain and assigned to take her to Baltimore. On board also were Chief Engineer I. R. Dryburgh and Assistant Engineers F. H. Pulsifer and Walter Scott, all Revenue Marine Service men. The Baltimore Collector was ordered by Chase to pay the expenses of crew and officers and supply rations while she was in Chesapeake Bay. She arrived in Baltimore late in March. On April 1, Assistant Secretary Harrington wired the Baltimore Collector, saying:

> "Is she ready to sail? Can the Secretary see her if he comes over this afternoon? Is the gun on board."[12]

On April 24, Captain Shippen went back to New York and Lieutenant D. C. Constable took command. He was ordered to report to Flag Officer Goldsborough in command of the Atlantic Blockading Squadron at Hampton Roads. Shippen was thanked by Chase for his "prompt and important services."

Constable, no doubt chosen by Captain Faunce, had been in the service since 1852, and had been Faunce's Second Lieutenant on the *Harriet Lane*. He reported to Goldsborough April 29 and was almost immediately sent into action.[13]

Five weeks earlier, the Confederate ironclad *Merrimack* had steamed down the Elizabeth River and out to Hampton Bay to attack the Union fleet. The frigates *Cumberland* and *Congress* were destroyed and others damaged. The whole Bay area was in shock lest the new monster continue on to shell Washington.

The next day, the Union's ironclad *Monitor* appeared. After a battle that lasted all morning, both vessels retreated. There had been no further engagements by the time the *Stevens* appeared in Hampton Roads late in April.

Goldsborough ordered the *Stevens* to anchor next to the *Monitor*. On several occasions, the *Stevens* was sent to the mouth of the Elizabeth River to entice the *Merrimack* to come out and do battle. On one occasion when she appeared to be coming out to meet the challenge, Constable fired three shots at her. All three fell short, but the *Merrimack* turned and went back up the river.[14]

The Hoboken ironclad continued to assist Goldsborough during the dramatic week of May 5 when President Lincoln and Secretaries Stanton and Chase appeared to hasten the capture of Norfolk. A week after the city was taken, she was ordered to go with a Navy fleet, including the *Monitor*, up the James River to attach Richmond. All went well until the vessels reached the well-manned batteries at Drewry's Bluff, almost within sight of Richmond. Here, although shot bounced off the *Stevens'* iron sides, her guns could not be elevated to reach the batteries at the top of the bluff. In addition, her big West Point gun exploded when it was fired. Miraculously no one was killed or injured but the *Stevens* with the rest of the fleet returned to Hampton Bay, mission not accomplished. [15]

The Norfolk episode may have been too much for Constable. His health failed, and on May 29, he was detached from *Stevens* and assigned to special duty in New York. In 1863 he was delegated to supervise the building of new steam cutters for the service. [16]

In November 1862 the *Stevens* was ordered to stand guard at Throggs Neck at the Long Island Sound entrance to New York Harbor. She remained there until the following February when she was ordered to the Narrows to guard the seaward entrance to the harbor. In July 1863 she towed the schooner *Varina* to Philadelphia via Cape May. [17]

About this time Secretary Chase ordered that her name be changed back to the original *"Naugatuck"* on the recommendation of her officers. This seems to have caused some concern in New York for, on December 13, 1863, Barney received the following letter from the Treasury Department:

"In regard to the Revenue Cutter called Naugatuck by the officers in command I have to say that the former name, viz E. A. Stevens is the proper name and only one recognized by the department. [18]

Back at Throggs Neck in August 1863, a terrible explosion occurred when the pivot gun was being tested. The breech of the gun burst and went through the wheelhouse and cabin, severely injuring Lieutenant George Walden, son of the renouned, retired Captain Green Walden, and six other men. She was hastily repaired and continued on duty, her men inspecting about 62 vessels a day. She remained at Throggs Neck for the rest of the war, except for short intervals when she relieved *Miami* at the Narrows. Late in 1865 she was ordered to New Bern, North Carolina. She spent the rest of her days in New Bern, Baltimore and Norfolk until she was sold to Henry Brown in Baltimore April 24, 1890 for $3,025. [19]

CHAPTER XIV

More New Revenue Cutters

In 1863, two more steam cutters were purchased and six were built under the supervision of Thomas B. Stillman, formerly a clerk in the New York office of the auditor of the Treasury Department and now Supervising Inspector of Steam Cutters. He worked closely with Collector Barney and Barney's successor, Simeon Draper, and with Assistant Treasury Secretary Harrington.

This stepped-up program was in answer to the increase in rebel privateering along the coast. All the new cutters were to cooperate with the Navy as ordered by Lincoln in a directive to Secretary Chase June 14, 1863. He authorized Chase to

> cooperate by the revenue cutters under your direction with the Navy in arresting rebel depredation on American commerce and transportation and in capturing rebels engaged therein.[1]

Cuyahoga

Of the vessels purchased in 1863, *Cuyahoga* was a 305-ton propeller steamer, the former *Santa Anna*.[2] She had an interesting history. Built for the Mexican Navy by J. A. and D. D. Westervelt in New York, she was the sister ship of a vessel in the United States Navy. Her Mexican commander stole her from his country and turned her into a slaver. As a slaver she was chased and attacked by her sister ship, which sank in the battle. Her owners continued to operate her as a slave ship until, needing repairs, she was disguised and brought into New York. When her owners could not pay the repair bill she was seized by the United States, auctioned at Philadelphia and bought by the Secretary of the Treasury for a revenue cutter in April 1863 at a cost of $25,000. Captain McGowan was detailed to command her. On June 25 she was ordered to Port Royal to cooperate with the Navy in searching for "pirates."[2] In July she was ordered north from Hilton Head with mail for New York. Arriving during the bloody draft riots in the city, she was towed to Jersey City and then to Tarrytown to escape injury. A black steward from the Treasury office in New York was taken aboard to save his life.[3]

In August she made a cruise to New England, stopping at Nauset, Cape Cod, and proceeding to East Boston, Portland, Monhegan Island, Matinicus, and Eastport, where she joined the cutter *Black* and was visited by Assistant Treasury Secretary Harrington.

In September she was hit by a ferry boat in New York Harbor and laid up for repairs. In December she was sent to Long Branch on the Jersey coast to assist the stranded Italian frigate *Red Italia*, and in January and February 1864, she cruised between New York and Fernandina, Florida, in search of blockade runners and rebel privateers. In February she took Special Treasury Agent A. G. Browne from Port Royal to Fernandina, and on February 8, seized the *Pride of the Sea* and brought her back to Port Royal. Captain McGowan consulted with Admiral Dahlgren USN on the *U.S.S. Vermont* at Hilton Head and received more arms for *Cuyahoga*. She then proceeded to Beaufort, North Carolina, where rebel attacks were feared.

Cruising off Cape Henlopen, March 13, 1864, she was run into by an unknown steamer and was considerably damaged. Repairs at the Philadelphia Navy Yard cost $30,699. She was laid up until September when she was sent to New York and then ordered to resume cruising between New York and Florida. In December she was sent to Sag Harbor and Edgartown. Late that month Captain McGowan was ordered to the *Nemaha*. He was replaced by Captain Faunce. The cutter was then ordered to Savannah, but for some reason did not go. She was in New York when the war ended.[4]

She remained in the service to make a sentimental voyage to Havana in 1867 under the command of Captain Faunce to retrieve the *Harriet Lane* which had been captured by the rebels in 1863 and taken to Havana.[5] *Cuyahoga* was sold soon after in New York for $31,400.[6]

Pawtuxet

First of the six new steam cutters in 1863 was the *Pawtuxet* built at the yard of Thomas Stark in New York. She slid down the ways July 7, 1863. She drew 4 feet 5 inches forward and 5 feet 10 inches aft.[7] She was "named in honor of the River which furnishes the greatest motive power for the manufactories of Rhode Island," and christened by Collector Barney "in the absence of Miss Chase." In June 1864 she was commanded by Lieutenant Amazeen, with William E. Hollaway and James H. Wicks as his junior lieutenants. Captain Alvan A. Fengar assumed command in October and was ordered to take the cutter to Boston. She remained there throughout the war, assisting the sailing cutter *Morris* in cruising from Portsmouth, New Hampshire, to New Bedford, Massachusetts, as part of the Atlantic Blockade.

In November 1864, when Lincoln was up for re-election, she was ordered to Gloucester, Massachusetts, and her men were sent ashore "to guard the Customs House, it being voting day." Several times she served as an ice-breaker in Boston and Gloucester harbors.

In 1866 she was detailed to winter cruising of Massachusetts under Captain Fengar. A detailed chart shows that she cruised 3,654 miles, 631 under steam, 943 under steam and sail, and 2,080 under canvas from January to May; boarded 47 vessels; assisted 9 vessels in distress and burned 112 tons of coal.[8]

Laid up and dismantled May 3, 1867, she was sold August 9 to P. L. Everett of Boston for $25,600.[9]

Ashuelot

The day after the *Pawtuxet* was launched, the *Ashuelot* went down the ways at the Eglis yard, also in New York. She was a 323-ton steamer, drawing 4 feet 8 inches forward and 6 feet 8 inches aft. She cost about $103,000.[10] On December 21, 1864, she was ordered to Eastport, Maine, to assist the *Black* in patrolling the Canadian border. First commanded by Captain Usher, she was turned over to Captain Merryman when she went to Charleston, South Carolina, in December 1866 to replace the *Kewanee*. On April 27, 1867, she was laid up at Staten Island, New York,[11] and sold to J. C. Fuller and Brother who registered her July 26.[12]

Mahoning (Levi Woodbury) in Two Wars

Next of the new steam cutters to be launched was the 130 foot *Mahoning*, one of the longest-lived vessels in the entire service. She was to remain on duty, mainly in New England waters, until August 10, 1915 — long enough to witness the change of name of the service from "Revenue Cutter Service" to "United States Coast Guard."

Contracted for by J. M. Lynn and Sons at Reid Street, Philadelphia, in 1863 as Revenue Cutter Number Five, she cost $92,000. She was built under the supervision of Captain David Constable, who had commanded *E. A. Stevens* in her dramatic episodes in Hampton Bay and at Drewrys Bluff. She was 130 feet long, 27 feet wide, with a depth of 11 1/2 feet. She drew 5 feet forward and 5 feet 4 inches aft.[13] Launched July 9, 1863, and christened by the Philadelphia Collector's daughter Rebecca Thomas, she was ordered to Portland, Maine, July 19 to assist the sail cutter *Dobbin* under command of Captain John A. Webster, Jr. She eventually replaced the *Dobbin* at Portland in January 1865.

When she first arrived at Portland, Captain Usher of the *Dobbin* gave her a pilot and ten men to assist her in searching for rebel cruisers. Both cutters did extensive cruising until war's end.[14] On June 5, 1873, the *Mahoning's* name was changed to *Levi Woodbury* in honor of the American jurist and statesman who had died in 1851.

The *Mahoning* continued to cruise in New England until 1898 when she was ordered to join the Navy at Havana in the Spanish-American War. She was the only cutter to serve in both the Civil War and the Spanish-American War. She returned to Maine in 1898 and remained in that area until 1915. After 52 years of service the cutter was sold to Thomas Butler of 15-23 Medford Street, Boston, for $4,286 August 10, 1915.[15]

Wayanda

Built by Fardy and Brother at Baltimore, the *Wayanda*, (originally called "Wawayanda"), cost $103,000.[16] She was launched September 1, 1863 and christened by the Baltimore Collector's 8-year-old daughter, Betsy Hoffman. She was ordered to Washington Navy Yard the following May under command of Captain John J. White. Her first assignment was to take Governor and Mrs. Sprague and friends on an overnight cruise along the Potomac. As they passed Mount Vernon, they "half-masted the colors and tolled the bell." En route they were joined by the cutter *Tiger* with Assistant Treasury Secretary Harrington on board. He joined them on the *Wayanda*.

Ten days later Captain White was ordered to take Mrs. Sprague to Newport. In August, the *Wayanda* went to New York and was put into a drydock in Brooklyn for repairs. On February 2, 1865, there was a change of command, Captain Faunce taking the helm briefly until Captain Merryman arrived to take the cutter to Port Royal to join the Cotton Fleet. On February 6, *Wayanda* and *Kewanee* crossed the bar off Port Royal together and communicated with Admiral Dahlgren. They were ordered to convoy 24 cotton vessels to New York, leaving February 8.

The *Wayanda*, whose number in the fleet was 23, (which she carried at the fore) outpaced the fleet and was well ahead, even of the flagship *U.S.S. Flag*, by nightfall. The *Kewanee* too was in the lead but the fleet was scattered in a severe storm—"snowing and blowing strong"—halfway up the coast. The *Wayanda* reached port with split sails February 14. All the vessels were considerably damaged by the gale, including the *Kewanee* which failed to appear in New York until February 19.

The cutter convoyed a second fleet to New York in March, leaving Savannah March 16 and arriving March 19. She was then ordered to remain at Staten Island to protect the huge quantities of cotton piled up in warehouses at the Quarantine Station. She was there April 19 when word of Lincoln's assassination was received. Merryman ordered the colors set at half mast, and the yards cock-billed. That is to trim the yards by the lifts in a diagonal manner. All work was suspended that day and the next. They fired 36 minute guns as a tribute to the late President.

In May 1865 the *Wayanda* was sent to Fortress Monroe where Salmon P. Chase, now Chief Justice, came on board with a party of dignitaries to tour the conquered South. They took a special pilot on board and left May 2, reaching Beaufort, North Carolina, three days later. They next visited Fort Fisher but did not go up to Wilmington, North Carolina. On the tenth they

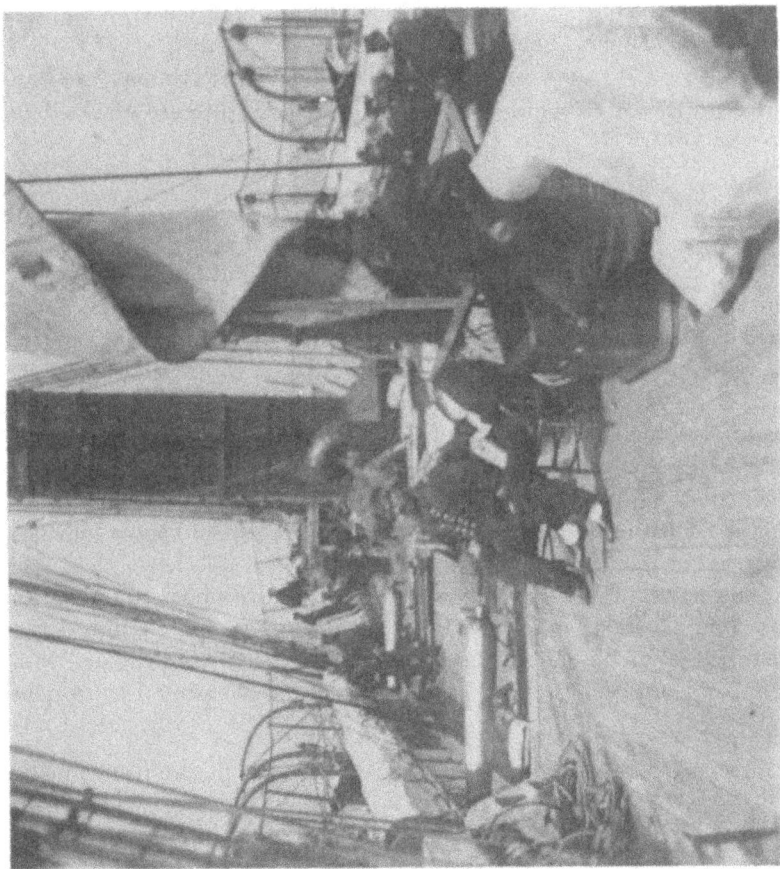

President Lincoln (standing), Secretary of State Seward
and Captain John White on board the cutter *Wayanda*
Coast Guard Academy Library

14-5

were in Charleston, on the 12th at Hilton Head. At Hilton Head, Chase boarded the cutter *Nemaha* and went to Beaufort, South Carolina. He also visited Savannah.

The next leg of the voyage took them to Fernandina, Key West, Havana, Mobile, and New Orleans, where the Chief Justice left the cutter.

For a week they cruised in the Gulf of Mexico, visiting Pensacola and seizing a schooner for violation of the revenue laws. On July 30, 1865, the *Wayanda* was ordered from Key West to Aspinwall, Panama. She returned to New Orleans in August. In December, Captain Merryman was given command of the new cutter *Hugh McCullough* at New Orleans, and the *Wayanda* was ordered to Philadelphia. She reached there January 8, 1866.[17]

Later that year *Wayanda* was sent to the Pacific and was stationed at San Francisco. In 1868, 1869, and 1870, she made several cruises to Alaska. She was sold in 1873.[18]

Kankakee

Kankakee was launched September 15 at the J. A. and D. D. Westervelt yard in New York. There was quite a celebration at her launching which was attended by Harrington, Barney, Stillman, Faunce, Constable, and Fengar, as well as the American consul at Rome. The vessel was christened with champagne by Barney's daughter, Susie.[19] *Kankakee* was a 350-ton brig-rigged steam cutter with two oscillating low pressure engines of 36 inch cylinder, 36 inch stroke. She carried a 30-pounder rifled Parrott gun and six 24-pounder howitzers.

Little is known of her early activities since there are no known journals in existence for the 1863-1865 period.

Late in the war, the *Kankakee* was sent to Savannah under command of Captain John G. Baker to convoy confiscated cotton from the South to the Quarantine Station on Staten Island, New York. Baker was delighted with his command. On February 5, 1865 he wrote the Treasury Department saying:

> This splendid little steamer arrived at Port Royal on the 3rd having made the passage from New York (off Jersey City) to Hilton Head in 67 running hours.[20]

After the war, she was sent to Mobile, Alabama, and then to Charleston and Norfolk. In 1866 she was laid up at Staten Island and sold June 20 to Wetmore Cryder and Company. She was registered in New York for merchant trade July 26.[21]

Kewanee

The *Kewanee* was built by J. A. Robb and Company, Baltimore, and launched September 23.[22] She was a 135-foot steam cutter with a single cylinder and a single screw. She measured 236 tons. She was stationed at New York later that year.

On August 16, 1864, Captain William Cooke Pease took command of the *Kewanee* at her wharf in Hoboken, New Jersey, opposite Manhattan. He spent a week getting her ready to cruise through Long Island Sound to New England in search of rebel privateers. They cruised as far as Boston where the *Kewanee* met her counterpart, the *Mahoning,* and challenged her to a race. The cutters left Boston Harbor at 10 A.M. and headed towards the Cape Ann Lighthouse. The turning point was the point at which the lighthouse bore due north, at which time each cutter fired a gun and reversed course. The distance was 55 miles. Some records say that the *Mahoning* won by four seconds; others that the *Kewanee* won by seven seconds. At any rate, it was close when they crossed the finish line at Fort Independence, Boston.[23]

Back in New York October 25, the cutter was once more ordered to cruise from New York to Boston. In January 1865, she was sent to Port Royal to meet and convoy 26 cotton-laden vessels escorted by the *U.S.S. Flag.*

On the way north, a severe storm broke up the cotton fleet and sent the *Kewanee* off course and into Newport with a half-frozen crew and a damaged keel. She returned hastily to New York but had to break her way through the ice in Long Island Sound and stop for repairs before she docked at her usual place at Hoboken. She was almost immediately sent to Port Royal again to convoy another Cotton Fleet. Later that year she spent some time guarding the cotton at the Quarantine Station at Staten Island before it was auctioned off to pay war debts. She was then assigned to guard duty at the entrance to New York Harbor.

In July she took Stillman on a tour of inspection of the revenue cutters along the New England coast. They stopped at Newport where they picked up Chief Justice Chase and the Honorable Samuel Hooper for a cruise under sail on Block Island Sound, with some fishing off Point Judith. While underway under steam on the way home, they met the British steam yacht *Octavia* and challenged her to a race. The *Wayanda* crossed the *Octavia's* bow before they reached Newport.

Putting the Chief Justice and his friends on shore, they continued on to New Bedford, Woods Hole, Martha's Vineyard, Pollock Rip Lightship, Handkerchief Lightship, Monomoy Light, Chatham Light, Nauset Light, Highland Light, and Boston Light. The cutter came to off India Wharf, Boston, where Superintendent Stillman transferred to the *Pawtuxet* for the rest of the voyage up the coast. The *Kewanee* returned to New York. Before she left she challenged the *Pawtuxet* to a race in Massachusetts Bay. She left her a mile astern and "fairly beaten." On the way to New York, she stopped for a few hours in Edgartown, Massachusetts, where Captain Pease went ashore to see his wife and son. *Kewanee* made the voyage from Edgartown to Hoboken in 31 hours and 15 minutes.

The *Kewanee* was next ordered to Charleston where Captain Pease had been stationed twice in the 1840's and 1850's. She spent some time in both Charleston and Savannah, and was then ordered to search the coast from Savannah to Fernandina for smugglers and others violating the revenue laws. In December, at Charleston, the Captain was stricken with typhoid fever.

He died on board the cutter December 30. His place was taken by the next in command, Lieutenant Joseph Irish, and later by Captain James Selden. The *Kewanee* was next sent to Key West. In 1866 she was ordered to New York where she was laid up at Staten Island[24] and sold July 10, 1867 for $25,100. She was then registered for foreign trade.[25]

Bronx

Late in 1863, a 187 ton steam boat named the *Addison F. Andrews* was purchased by Stillman and re-named *Bronx*. She had been built in Brooklyn that year and registered for coastwise trade. Her owner sold her to the Revenue Cutter Service on December 5 for $42,000. She became the work-horse of New York Harbor, constantly towing the sailing cutters from place to place and even occasionally towing some of the steam cutters. She remained in the service until the end of the war. Her further history is not known, but she was still in the service in 1871.[26] When she was wrecked at Port Penn, Pennsylvania, that year she was under the command of Captain Webster, Jr.

CHAPTER XV

Cutters in Combat in 1864

Nemaha, under her former name *Flora,* had served with the Army at Port Royal soon after the port was captured by the Union on November 7, 1861. After a year in the South she returned to New York for repairs which cost over $30,000. In 1864 she was named "Nemaha" and ordered back to Port Royal under command of young First Lieutenant Samuel B. Warner, with a crew of fourteen, to work with the Army. She stood into Port Royal Harbor June 16.[1] On the following day she seized the bark *Lindia* from Philadelphia with coal for the Navy, and after a search, turned her over to the Customs collector at Hilton Head under suspicion of having smuggled goods on board. Warner worked under the direction of the Collector for the rest of the month. He boarded and searched all incoming and departing vessels, and serviced the Martins Industry Lightship.[2]

On July 1 *Nemaha* "hauled alongside the wharf" at Beaufort and received rations and baggage for General Rufus Saxton and his staff. The General and staff arrived that afternoon and were immediately taken on board at Hilton Head. En route *Nemaha* aided the steamer *Mary Boardman* which was stuck on a sand bar. The following day General Saxton and his staff were taken to Edisto where they exchanged places with General James D. Foster and his staff who were then taken to Stono. At Stono *Nemaha* picked up 8 barges loaded with troops and towed them back to Edisto, training her guns on shore to cover the troops when they went ashore late that afternoon.

On July 3 she was under attack while assisting land forces. She fired back at the battery with her bow gun, a 20-pounder Parrott rifle, using all her ammunition after firing 60 rounds. Her commander then borrowed a 12-pounder Dahlgren gun and ammunition from the nearby steamer *Croton* and proceeded to assist more troops in landing. In the later part of July *Nemaha* was back at Hilton Head and Commander Warner was again taking his orders from the Customs Collector. On July 26 he took a special agent from the Treasury Department to Fernandina, Florida. En route *Nemaha* was fired on by a Navy gunboat until she made her identity known by burning a blue signal light. She boarded several vessels along the way. Upon her return she was ordered to deliver 400 watermelons to the troops at Folley Island near Charleston.

The cutter spent much of her time in the late summer shuttling the 25 miles between Hilton Head and Beaufort. She always reported to the Customs collector when she reached Hilton Head, and seems to have taken most of her orders from him or from the Special Agent at this time. In November a new Special Agent, A. G. Browne, arrived and made good use of the cutter in visiting the local ports. There were now 25 men in the crew. On at least one occasion some of them were sent ashore to cut wood for the galley stove. *Nemaha* took on coal and water at Beaufort. Sometimes she was sent out to coastwise steamers in the harbor to pick up and dispatch mail. In late November she was again turned over to the Army.

On November 22 she went to Morris Island, off Charleston, with dispatches from General Foster. She made the voyage in a day returning to the Beaufort wharf that night. On November 26 she had General Saxton, Commander Lane of the *USS Constitution*, Agent Browne, three officers and 50 soldiers on board. Browne and Lane left the cutter at Beaufort. Warner was then ordered to take the officers and soldiers and some dispatches to Morris Island. The soldiers were landed at Stono Inlet the next morning. His next assignments were to deliver coal to the lightship on Rattle Snake Shoal and take General Hatch and his staff from the gunboat *Mary Sanford* to Hilton Head.

With Union forces under General Sherman advancing on Savannah, an all-out effort was now made to disrupt the railroad that linked Savannah and Charleston. General Foster was ordered to move troops up the Broad River to Boyds Landing from which position they would advance to destroy an important bridge on the railroad. He chose *Nemaha* as his flagship, bringing his staff on board November 28 and hoisting his flag at her peak. She was then ordered to move out into the fleet he had assembled on Port Royal Sound and "signalize" the vessels that the attack was underway.

It was a foggy night and two of the Army steamers, *Cosmopolitan* and *Delaware*, soon went aground, *Nemaha* pulled them into deep water. By then she had lost the fleet. In trying to find it, her pilot, a negro, went up the wrong river. As Commander Warner said in the Journal: "he did not know where we were." They then turned around and cruised down the river, finding the rest of the expedition waiting at Bay Point. The pilot found he had gone up the Chickasee River instead of the Broad River.

Nemaha next cruised up the Broad River and found the *Cosmopolitan* aground again. After she pulled her off, the cutter proceeded to Boyds Landing where the troops were being landed. *Delaware* went aground again and had to be assisted in getting off. Lieutenant Everett Webster was then assigned to transfer *Delaware's* troops to the steamer *Wyoming*. After this busy day *Nemaha* returned to Hilton Head with General Foster and his staff for the night. The General and his staff returned on board at 8 A.M. the next morning to be taken back to Boyds Landing. They reached there at 10:40 A.M. to find the steamer *Cosmopolitan* aground for the third time. After she was afloat, *Nemaha* went down the river to find the troop ship *Philadelphia* and tow her to the landing.[3]

On the following morning, December 1, the *Nemaha* had direct encounter with the enemy when she left Boyds Landing and steamed up the Coosawhackey River to shell a rebel battery while the troops marched on to attack the rebel forces along the railroad. As her Journal reports:

Thursday, December 1, 1864

Commences light breeze from the N.W. and clear At 7:30 weaighed anchor and Steamed up the "river" to enter "Coosawhackey river, and "Shelled" a rebel Battary on the "Port" Side of the "river" firing "Seventy Seven (77) Rounds" having cleared them out the "Battary" ceased fireing. "Seeing two "Negro Boys" in the marsh Sent a boat, and brought them on board. at 2 P.M. sent a boat with "Lieut Webster to Sound up the "Fullafinny river" as far as possible. he sounded up the river to within six hundred yards of the enemy's "Battary, Surprised a Rebel Picket Station Boat" then returned to the "Vessel" Got underway and Steamed down the river arriving at Boyd Landing at 6:47 P.M. anchored in the Stream and communicated with the Shore, "At 12 midnight calm with fog, this day ends the same "Shiped S. March, Mr. Guinnis "Boy" Served 27 rations to the crew, and two rations to the Negro Boys & one the Pilot. 272 Rations on hand the 1st day of December 1864."[4]

Early December 2 she took on board the 25th Ohio Regiment and with General Foster in command, steamed up Whale Branch Creek to flush out any rebels that might be there. The morning fog was so thick that navigation on the creek was impossible. She was ordered to return to Boyds Landing and disembark the troops. She returned later to Hilton Head, and General Foster and his staff went ashore.

They returned the next day, bringing 127 rounds of ammunition back to Boyds Landing where they again picked up the 25th Ohio and proceeded up Whale Branch Creek. At Pages Point they landed the troops and then "dropped down" to the Port Royal Ferry dock. Ranging their guns on shore, General Foster sent an armed party ashore to scout the road. At 6:20 P.M. the armed party and the troops returned on board, having captured two pieces of artillery. The troops were taken back to Boyds Landing on *Nemaha*. One piece of the artillery was towed on a scow behind the cutter.

On December 5, *Nemaha* left Boyds Landing at 9:15 and steamed up the Coosawhackey River to join the gun boat *Daffodil* and the steamer *Plato* in attacking "Dawson's Rebel Battary." After *Nemaha* fired 25 rounds of shot and shell she was obliged to go to the assistance of *Plato,* disabled by a shot that struck her cylinder. She towed *Plato* back to Boyds Landing. The next morning she took a company of infantry with horses to the Fullafinney River, landing them on Gregory's Plantation. From morning until midnight she ferried troops from Boyds Landing to the plantation and towed boats with army equipment by order of General Foster.

Among the items captured were sixteen barrels of whiskey which were shared by *Nemaha* and the steamer *Canonicus*. This must have helped the men on *Nemaha* get through what was a long day. After leaving the plantation, the cutter returned to Hilton Head, where General Foster and his staff disembarked. She was next sent out to the schooner *Plandome* from New York to take on board 618 Navy rations, and then ordered to St. Helena Sound to have her boiler repaired. The intense firing at Gregory's Plantation had loosened the rivets in her boiler and "set it to leaking." She reached the Sound at midnight.

It took just a day to repair the boiler. The following day, with Treasury Agent Browne on board, *Nemaha* took 3,000 feet of lumber on board and delivered it to a military outpost on the Fullafinney River.

General Foster returned on board the next day and hoisted his flag. The cutter made a trip to Gregory's Plantation to deliver three barrels of whiskey and then anchored in the Coosawhackey. After delivering another three barrels to Colonel Place the next day, she steamed back to Hilton Head and immediately left for Fort Pulaski and Savannah, arriving there at 1:30 P.M. Here, after communicating with Admiral Dahlgren commanding the Navy fleet, the cutter took on board three scouts from General Sherman's forces and left for Ossabaw Sound and the Ogeechee river.

At 5:20 P.M. General Foster was in communication with the gun boat *Flag* and put one of the scouts, a signal officer, on board. They then steamed for Warsaw Sound where they communicated with the iron clad *USS Passaic*. By midnight they were anchored in the Wilmington River.[5]

General Sherman on Board

The next day they returned to Fort Pulaski and then to Hilton Head arriving at 6:20 P.M. An hour later they were on their way back to the Ogeechee River. At 1:10 A.M. they communicated with the *Flag* and found that General Sherman had captured Fort McAllister on the Ogeechee River. Steaming up the river, they anchored off Fort McAllister at 7 A.M. December 14. Almost immediately General Sherman came on board to be taken to Admiral Dahlgren on the flagship *Philadelphia*. They put him on board and later returned and took him back to Fort McAllister. *Nemaha* then went back to Hilton Head, where General Foster and his staff went ashore at 5 P.M. The cutter went on to Beaufort and took on 20 tons of coal and 200 gallons of water. It was near midnight — a calm and clear midnight — when they finished.

By 9:15 the next morning, they were back at Hilton Head for General Foster and his staff and on their way to Ossabaw Sound where they took the Admiral off the *USS Harvest Moon* and up the Ogeechee River to Savannah. A boat was sent to sound the river and remove obstructions. At the Savannah and Gulf railroad bridge they picked up General Howard of General Sherman's forces and six river pilots to be taken aboard six Army transports. After delivering the pilots they took the mail from Sherman's army back to Hilton Head to be sent north.

With the fighting over in Georgia late in December 1864, Treasury Agent Browne demanded the use of the cutter, transporting his wife, friends and horses from port to port. Commander Warner was not pleased with his new orders—especially when he was obliged to transport the agent's horse, or delay a cruise because the wife of a friend of the agent "thought the weather was not fit to go out."

On December 26, the day after Savannah surrendered to Union forces, *Nemaha* took Browne and a party of friends from Hilton Head to view the fallen city. With a number of passengers on board the cutter reached Savannah at 4:30 P.M. and remained overnight at a wharf. She had two minor accidents en route, one at Hilton Head where the *George Leary* ran into her starboard wheel house, and one in the Savannah River where the *Canonicus* stove in her port wheel house.

After a night in Savannah she was ordered to take a Customs collector and a number of other passengers to Fernandina. After a rough voyage she landed her passengers at Fernandina and returned to Savannah. The next morning (New Year's Day, 1865) she was ordered to return to Hilton Head with Agent Browne, Mrs. Browne, Collector Severance, other passengers and two horses.

This was to be Commander Warner's last day on *Nemaha*. He was ordered to Boston to serve on the sailing cutter *Morris*. When the cutter reached Hilton Head her new commander, Captain McGowan, came on board. McGowan had been patrolling from Hatteras to Fernandina in *Cuyahoga*.[6]

Captain McGowan at Savannah

Nemaha now spent most of her time in the Savannah River, guiding vessels through the obstructions and towing them off sand bars. Other cutters appeared—*Kankakee, Kewanee,* and *Wayanda*. Captain McGowan also did a considerable amount of entertaining at Savannah. On January 12 and 13 he hosted dinners for the Secretary of War Edwin Stanton, Treasury Agent Simeon Draper and six generals—Sherman, Foster, Meigs, Baird, Barnes and Townsend. On January 14 he took the Secretary of War to Hilton Head. Draper remained on board while assembling the Cotton Fleet to take confiscated cotton to New York.

The cutter towed some of the cotton loaded vessels to the armed vessels that were to convoy them up the coast in February.

Another fleet of cotton vessels was assembled in March and sent North. In April, when word came that Lee had surrendered, *Nemaha* was at Fort Sumter with Collector Severance, his wife and invited guests on board. They had anchored overnight off the Battery and were taken to see what remained of Fort Sumter the next morning. They were later taken into Charleston where they spent the night. Meantime Captain McGowan was busy boarding and inspecting 15 vessels in Charleston Harbor with cargoes for the Charleston Quartermaster. The cutter returned to Hilton Head April 17.

They were anchored off Land's End April 18 when they heard "the melancholy news of the assasination of the President of the U.S." On board the boatswain, the coxswain and a seaman welcomed the news and made disparaging remarks about Lincoln. All three were placed in double irons and on April 21, put in prison in Savannah where they remained for several months.

Late in April *Nemaha* was used to transport the rebel prisoner, G. B. Lamar, and his daughter from Savannah to Hilton Head. The cutter remained in the South until the end of June 1865 when she arrived at Baltimore for repairs.[7] She later served at Norfolk in Mother Hawkin's Hole, and was burned to the water's edge under questionable circumstances in February 1868 at the mouth of the Wicomico River, Chesapeake Bay.[8]

Gunfire on Tibbots Creek

Captain Thomas M. Dungan was on an errand of mercy when he left Point Lookout on Chesapeake Bay August 12, 1864 and headed south in the cutter *Reliance* for the Great Wicomico River. He had been asked by a Mr. Appleby, a refugee from the hotbed of rebels along the Wicomico, to bring his children to northern territory. They were to be waiting for *Reliance* on Tibbots Creek, one of the tributaries that flowed into the Wicomico.[9]

It was a dangerous area but Captain Dungan and *Reliance* were accustomed to visiting dangerous territories. For more than a year Dungan had been cruising in the lower Chesapeake where goods were constantly being smuggled to rebel forces defending Richmond. He had seized a number of log canoes and small schooners and sloops carrying contraband and dispatches, and he had rescued several persons, white and black, fleeing from rebel territory.[10]

Reliance and her sister cutter *Hercules* took orders from both the Baltimore Collector and the Army at Norfolk. They were not subject to Navy orders and, in fact, found themselves competing with the Potomac Flotilla of the Navy in 1864.

Captain Dungan complained to Secretary Chase that the Potomac Flotilla had ordered the *Reliance* and *Hercules* to stay out of their territory. He said they had been told by officers of the Flotilla that they would be seized "if found in the waters of western Virginia."[11] The Baltimore Collector then sent Captain J. M. Jones in the *Tiger* to the Rappanhannock River. The Flotilla officers refused to discuss the matter, but when it was brought to the attention of the Navy Secretary he said "no such order" had ever been issued. This was good news to the revenue cutter men for they received a small amount of prize money for every rebel vessel seized and adjudicated.

Reliance had seized a small sloop *Union* and sent her to Baltimore for adjudication. She had captured a log canoe with seven barrels of whiskey on board, and had taken the three men on board as prisoners to Point Lookout. On one occasion, Dungan sent his men ashore on Mill Creek to investigate rumors that rebel cavalry was "prowling about the neighborhood." He also seized several vessels loaded with coal for rebel steamers.

Many of *Reliance's* missions were charitable. She often took aboard stranded negroes fleeing from their masters, and once picked up a rebel whose home was in Union territory. She took him to Annapolis, where he swore allegiance to the United States before a judge. *Reliance* then returned him to his family. She had reunited families divided by the war, one of them the Kent family. Mrs. Kent and her child were picked up on the Great Wicomico River and taken to Annapolis to join Mr. Kent.[12]

On August 12, 1864 *Reliance* left Point Lookout at 8:55 A.M. and by 10:30 had passed Smith's Point Lighthouse. She stopped shortly after so Captain Dungan could communicate with the men on the lightship off Smith's Point. At meridian she steamed up the Great Wicimico, coming to anchor off Tibbots Creek in 15 feet of water. A boat was sent ashore, under Lieutenant Henry D. Hall, to find the Appleby children and bring them back to the cutter. The boat returned without the children.

Meantime a number of unfriendly people congregated on shore near a fleet of canoes. Captain Dungan thought it wise to "secure" the canoes to "prevent their use by persons whom we saw collecting on the shore." Coxswain G. W. Agus and four ordinary seamen, Sam Lewis, Peter Cooper, Eli Cantley and David Smithers were sent ashore in a boat to get the canoes. Two canoes were brought to the cutter but when the men went back for the third they were fired on and captured.

Captain Dungan then opened fire on the shore, using *Reliance's* small pivot gun and small arms. More and more belligerents gathered on shore. Since he did not have enough men or ammunition to confront "the guerillas," Dungan decided to slip his anchor and get away. Almost as soon as he issued the order he was struck by a bullet and mortally wounded. At the same time Thomas Roberts, in charge of the pivot gun, was wounded.

The men continued to fire on shore as they turned the cutter in the river and headed down stream. They took Roberts to Point Lookout to have his wound dressed and then continued on to Baltimore where they landed the remains of "our gallant Captain."[13]

As far as can be determined from Civil War records, Captain Dungan was the only man in the Revenue-Cutter Service to lose his life in combat in the Civil War.

CHAPTER XVI

The Four Great Captains

In reviewing Revenue Cutter history during the Civil War period, the names of four officers stand out—Captains William A. Howard, John Faunce, John McGowan, and Douglass Ottinger. It was Howard's genius for organization that rescued the fragile service from the brink of disintegration in April 1861, and adapted it to serve the needs of both Army and Navy. It was Faunce, with his superior command of the *Harriet Lane,* who bolstered confidence in the cutters and their officers. McGowan had a remarkable ability for refitting old cutters and fitting out new ones to meet the demands of three Departments—Treasury, War, and Navy. As for Ottinger, his capability in handling all assignments, large and small, was remarkable. He put Lincoln ashore at Norfolk when that city was still in the hands of the Confederates; he shepherded five small cutters on a 2,300 mile voyage from the Great Lakes to the Atlantic in the dead of winter; he helped clear North Carolina's troubled inland waters of rebel and non-rebel law-breakers; he served with distinction as first president of the Examining Board that improved the caliber of Revenue Cutter officers, and he superintended the building of a steam cutter on the Great Lakes. In addition he helped to organize the Life-Saving Service.[1]

All these men had been long in the cutter service. Howard since 1829, McGowan and Ottinger since 1832, Faunce since 1837. They were to continue to play important roles in the post-war Revenue Marine, Howard in the early exploration and protection of Alaska, McGowan, Ottinger and Faunce in vessel construction, Life Saving Service and the training of young officers. These men were in the tradition of the great captains of the 1790s and early 1800s—John Foster Williams, Hopley Yeaton, Elisha Hinman, Patrick Dennis, Jonathan Maltbie, James Montgomery, Richard Taylor, David Porter, William Cooke, Robert Cochrane and John Howell.

Among the younger men, James H. Merryman and Charles G. Shoemaker went on to notable careers. Shoemaker, the young cadet who fought his way north to join Union forces when his cutter, *Lewis Cass,* was seized at Mobile, became Commandant of the service in the early 20th century.

In 1860 Treasury Secretary Cobb felt that the cutters were almost useless but his successor, the wizard of finance, Secretary Chase, knew that he could not underwrite a war without their help. To Secretary Chase, his assistant George Harrington, and the Customs Collectors (especially Collector Barney of New York) go a great deal of credit for revitalizing the service in its essential work in the collection of the revenue, and for increasing its value to both Army and Navy in the course of the war. To a lesser extent Stillman and Draper should be credited.

In addition to the Revenue Cutter officers and to the government officials, the war could not have been successfully concluded without the assistance of the thousands of ordinary seamen, gunners, coxswains, marines, pilots, cooks, and boys who served aboard the Civil War Cutters.

Too old to take an active part in the Civil War, Captain Henry Hunter came out of retirement to command the *James Campbell* at New London and Throggs Neck. He died with his sea boots on in December 1861. Another old-timer, Captain John A. Webster, father of Captain John A. Webster Jr., begged to be reinstated in the service from which he had been long retired, but his pleas fell on deaf ears. On June 25, 1863, he wrote Secretary Chase from his home in Harford County, Maryland, saying:

> Sir: I find by the Public prints, the necessity of all persons able to offer their services, therefore I feel as I might yet be qualified to take a command, to offer my services once more, to defend the City of Baltimore, As the *aged citizens of that place* will testify I done so during the War of 1812 on the night of the 13 and 14 Sept. 1814.
>
> This is the third time I have applied for duty since I was placed on the retired list but no notice taken of my application.[2]

He signed himself "John A. Webster, U.S.R. Service."

By late 1864, it was evident that the war would soon be over. Savannah had at last fallen to Union forces; the Confederate cruiser *Alabama* had been sunk by the Union *Kearsarge;* six of the seceding states were overrun with Union soldiers. Some Southern ports, notably Charleston and Wilmington, North Carolina, still defied the Atlantic Blockade, and rebel privateers continued to plunder Union shipping but Grant and Sherman were camped on the doorsteps of Charleston, and Lee's defenses of Richmond were weakening. By September 1864 a limited amount of legitimate trade was permitted in some of the Southern ports, increasing the work of the cutters. Illegitimate trade flourished. Even Union Army supplies turned up for sale in Southern communities.

There was trouble in the Great Lakes too when "suspicious" vessels, flying the Confederate flag, were said to be ready to attack Johnson Island where rebel prisoners were being held. Major General Hitchcock of Sandusky urged that "no time be lost in putting afloat armed vessels upon Lake Ontario and speedily upon the other lakes too."[3] The British were ready to put armed vessels on the lakes, and Congress was considering a bill to build six armed cutters for the lakes when the affair was settled by diplomacy.

Secretary Chase resigned from the Treasury Department and became Chief Justice of the United States. His place was taken by William P. Fessenden. In New York Collector Hiram Barney was replaced by Simeon Draper, who was not only Collector, but also a special Treasury Agent to supervise the collection and sale of cotton confiscated in the South. Stillman continued as Supervising Inspector of Steam Cutters.

Before he left office in the Treasury Department, Chase sent the following message "to all cutter captains:"

> Very considerable amounts of foreign merchandise have been introduced into the United States during the past year & a large quantity of goods is now being purchased & shipped to be smuggled in.[4]

He urged the men to do their duty, saying:

> The circumstances under which the government is placed imperatively requires that this should no longer be permitted.[5]

With more smuggling foreseen as the Union struggled with reconstruction, several vessels were added to the cutter fleet in 1864, by order of the Treasury Department and under the supervision of Supervisor Stillman.

New Cutters in 1864

Antietam

A small topsail schooner with a centerboard, the *Antietam,* was purchased from Fardy and Brothers, Baltimore for $8,000, March 1, 1864.[6] She was stationed at the strategic port of Beaufort, North Carolina, close to Fort Macon, to check the constant flow of maritime traffic from the Atlantic Ocean to North Carolina's plentiful inland waterways. Although under Union control, this whole territory was riddled with defiant rebels and with an increasing number of Northern entrepreneurs.

Before she left Baltimore, *Antietam* was equipped with gear from the *Andrew Jackson,* including a 30-pounder Parrott gun weighing 3,490 pounds, six Sharp's rifles, six smooth-bore muskets, copper powder flasks, a set of Royer's signals and book, a set of charts for the Southern coast, a mahogany binnacle and compass, and pig ballast. *Jackson* was to have been withdrawn from the service but she remained on duty until October 1865.

On her way to Beaufort, *Antietam* lost her centerboard and was obliged to return to Baltimore for repairs. She reached Beaufort July 5 and immediately began boarding vessels, sometimes as many as 86 in one day. In August, 821 vessels were boarded. She remained there and in New Bern until the war ended. The highlights of her career were the seizure of a schooner off Roanoke Island in December 1864, and the capture of six blockade runners in the Pungo

River the following March. They carried bales of cotton, brandy, cotton cards and 100 pounds of bacon.

After the war, *Antietam* saw duty at New Bedford, Massachusetts, Brownsville, Texas, in the district of Brazos de Santiago, Indianola, Texas and Mobile, Alabama.[7] She was sold at Mobile for $2,800 in January 1871.[8]

Northerner (Ewing)

The *Northerner,* a steam cutter, was purchased by Stillman from S. Crary and Brothers at Baltimore April 18, 1864 for $60,000.[9] Fitted out at New York she was first commanded by Captain Benjamin J. Kellam in July. When suspected of disloyalty he was removed, and command was given to Captain Faunce. Kellam was later acquitted.

In addition to Captain Faunce, she was staffed by two lieutenants, a pilot, three engineers, three coal passers, a boatswain, a gunner, two quartermasters, a master-at-arms, two coxswains, ten seamen, three boys, a cabin steward, a wardroom steward, a cabin boy, a wardroom boy and a cook.

Northerner sailed August 11, 1864 for the Washington Navy Yard, arriving two days later. The next day she took Assistant Secretary of the Treasury Harrington and associates down the Potomac to visit *USS Roanoke* at Point Lookout. In September she took Harrington to Boston where she joined *Pawtuxet* and *Mahoning.* The three cutters raced in Massachusetts Bay to test their speed. Back in Washington October 14 she took Secretary of the Treasury Fessenden and associates to Norfolk, and up the James River. Testing her armament, she fired 2 Hotchkiss shells, 6 Boerman shells, 1 shrapnel, 2 blank cartridges, and 20 Spencer rifle metallic cartridges while in the river. On October 16 and 17 she took Brigadier General Ingalls and Lt. Col. Morton of the Army of the Potomac up the river. With Fessenden they went aboard General Butler's flagship. The following day they went to the front with General Grant. That night Fessenden entertained at dinner on *Northerner* Generals Grant, Meigs, Ingalls, Secretary of War Stanton, and Surgeon General Barnes.[10]

In December Faunce was detached from command and replaced by Lieutenant John A. Henriques. In January *Northerner* took the Secretary of War to Norfolk to confer with New York Collector Simeon Draper about confiscated cotton. In the Potomac she moved "under easy steam on account of the ice in the River." On her return, her waterline was planked to protect her from the ice. In March she was used to transport government officials, and in April celebrated the surrender of Lee's army with rockets and fireworks at the Washington Navy Yard. On April 19, at noon, she fired a national salute of 36 guns "in honor of Abraham Lincoln, Sixteenth President of the United States who died April 15th inst."

When the war ended, she took Chief Justice Chase and party up the James River to Richmond, "running under easy steam on account of obstructions." They remained there for ten days. Later that month she made another voyage to Richmond, taking 16 officials, and in June she took a party of 13 to the fallen city. During the summer she transported several government officials, taking the Secretary of State to Point Lookout, and the Secretary of War and General Speed to Cape May.

In October she was ordered to Wilmington, North Carolina, the first revenue cutter assigned to the city that had been the last to surrender to Union forces. On October 6 she was at the Wilmington Custom House Wharf. Two days later she steamed down the Cape Fear River to Smithville, encountering no resistance. She exercised her guns, boarded a number of vessels, assisted vessels in distress, and towed becalmed sailing vessels down the long river to the sea. On November 15 she went to the assistance of the steamer *Twilight*, aground off New Inlet Bar, rescuing a number of passengers, and removing mail, specie and baggage.[11]

In 1866 *Northerner* was ordered to Baltimore and command was given to Captain McGowan. In subsequent years she served in New York, Florida and Baltimore. Her name was changed to *Ewing* November 19, 1874 when she was ordered to cruise from Washington to Norfolk. Later she was transferred to the Executive Committee of the Army of the Potomac and used in Chesapeake Bay as a marine hospital for quarantine duty. She was sold at Baltimore April 8, 1895 for $1,000.[12]

William H. Seward

Built at Wilmington, Delaware, the steam cutter *William H. Seward* was purchased as a new vessel in June 1864 under the direction of Supervising Inspector Stillman.[13] She was commissioned in October and spent the rest of the year boarding vessels in Delaware River. In Philadelphia she tied up at either the Pine Street Wharf or Neafs and Levys Wharf, and in Wilmington at the 4th Street Wharf. When the war ended she was being repaired and painted in preparation for going on a cruise.

She was commanded by Captain Henry B. Nones who had been in the service since 1831 and had fought in the Mexican-American War. There were 19 in the crew.

Except for a brief assignment in New York, she remained on the Delaware until 1875 when she was ordered South. She was then stationed at a number of ports on the Gulf of Mexico until she was sold to Lee Kimball at Mobile, Alabama, January 15, 1879, for $2,800.[14]

Winslow and Hector

Existing records in the National Archives indicate that there was a cutter named either *Hector* or *Winslow* on the Great Lakes. Actually there were two cutters, *Winslow* chartered September 28, 1864 at Buffalo, New York, and *Hector*, chartered October 5, 1864 at Oswego, New York — both for one month. They were put in commission and armed by Captain Ottinger who was then superintending the construction of the *Commodore Perry* at Buffalo. Both were steam tugs and were assigned to prevent smuggling and watch for any Confederate activity on the lakes. They were chartered for $4,500 a month.[15]

On a stormy night in October, *Winslow* was wrecked while coming into the pier at Cleveland, Ohio. A dispatch from Captain Ottinger to Secretary of the Treasury Fessenden October 18 enclosed the following report from Cleveland's Customs Collector C. Metz Jr.:

> The Winslow last night [October 14] about 9 o'clock when coming into the Pier under charge of the pilot struck the Bar. All on board saved except 5 of the crew. Vessel an entire loss. Persons escaped saved nothing but the clothes they had on.[16]

Ottinger asked for a full month's pay for the crew and for the families of the five seamen who were lost.[17]

Hector was still waiting for armament when *Winslow* went down. Soon after she cruised to Sacketts Harbor, under command of Captain Stephen Cornell. Collector A. Van Dyck advised purchasing *Hector* but she was merely chartered for an extra month. She went out of commission December 5.[18]

The Cutters in 1865

When Lee surrendered in April 1865 there were 35 cutters in the Revenue-Cutter Service, eight of them under construction. Steamers outnumbered sailing vessels two to one. They were:

Ashuelot, steam, at Eastport, Maine

Jeremiah S. Black, sail, at Eastport, Maine

Mahoning (Levy Woodbury), steam, at Portland, Maine

Isaac Toucey, sail, at Castine, Maine

Pawtuxet, steam, at Boston, Massachusetts

Morris, sail, at Boston, Massachusetts

James C. Dobbin, sail, at Edgartown, Massachusetts

Jacob Thompson, sail, at Newport, Rhode Island

Miami, steam, at Newport, Rhode Island

James Campbell, sail, at New London, Connecticut

Kewanee, steam, at New York, New York

Kankakee, steam, at Savannah, Georgia

Wayanda, steam, at New York, New York

Cuyahoga, steam, at New York, New York (under repair)

E. A. Stevens (Naugatuk), steam, at Throggs Neck, New York

Varina, sail, at Perth Amboy, New Jersey

William H. Seward, steam, at Philadelphia, Pennsylvania

Andrew Jackson, sail, at Baltimore, Maryland

Northerner, steam, at Washington, District of Columbia

Reliance, steam, in lower Chesapeake Bay

Tiger, steam, in lower Chesapeake Bay

Philip Allen, sail, at Norfolk, Virginia

Walter B. Forward, sail, at Beaufort, North Carolina

Antietam, sail, at New Bern, North Carolina

Nemaha, steam, at Port Royal, South Carolina

Joseph Lane (Campbell), sail, at San Francisco, California

Shubrick, steam, en route to Alaska, under Navy orders

Salmon P. Chase, steam, at Buffalo (under construction)
John A. Dix, steam, at Buffalo (under construction)
William P. Fessenden, steam, at Cleveland (under construction)
Commodore Perry, steam, at Buffalo (under construction)
William H. Seward, steam, at Philadelphia (under construction)
Hugh McCulloch, steam, at Baltimore (under construction)
Lincoln, steam, at Baltimore (under construction)
Andrew Johnson, steam, at Buffalo (under construction)

After the war, five vessels were purchased from the Navy, making a total of 12 new cutters in service in 1865. The Navy vessels were

> *Juniper,* steam, sent to New York. (Name later changed to *Uno* and then *Peter G. Washington.*)
> *Wilderness,* steam, sent to New Orleans
> *Mocassin,* steam, sent to Wilmington, N.C.
> *Nansemond (Joseph Freeborn)* steam, sent to Savannah
> *Delaware,* steam, sent to Galveston

Winning the Peace

Having helped the Union win the war, it was now up to the Revenue Cutter Service to help win the peace. The most able officers were sent south to accomplish the difficult task of re-establishing Customs, maritime laws, and friendship in ports they had so recently sought to destroy. *Kewanee* was sent to Charleston under command of Captain Pease who had been stationed there in the 1840's. Captain Merryman went to New Orleans in *Wayanda;* Captain McGowan to Wilmington, North Carolina in *Northerner;* Captain Colesbury to Savannah in *Nansemond;* Captain Davis to Key West in *John A. Dix;* Captain Warner to Mobile in *Morris;* Lieutenant Walden to New Bern in *E. A. Stevens;* and Captain Baker in *Kankakee* to Mobile and Charleston. It was not long before it was business as usual at southern customhouses and in southern waters.

Footnotes

Chapter I—On the Eve of Secession

1. Congressional Record 12.Stat. L.639. Feb. 4, 1863
2. Emily Steere, *Martha's Vineyard During the Civil War*. Mss. Dukes County Historical Society, Edgartown, Mass., 1960
3. *Battles and Leaders of the Civil War*. Grant-Lee Edition. New York: Century Co., 1884-1887. Vol. 1, p. 634
4. Charleston Daily Courier. Charleston, S.C. Feb. 25, 1861
5. Alexander Fraser, *Annual Report to the Secretary of the Treasury*, 1846
6. Captain Stephen H. Evans, *United States Coast Guard, A Definitive History*. United States Naval Institute, Annapolis, Md. 1939. p. 36
7. Ibid p. 35
8. Ibid p. 51
9. Ibid p. 87
10. Ibid p. 86
11. Journal of *Harriet Lane,* March 11, 1858
12. Evans, p. 65
13. Treasury Department Annual Report, 1860
14. Ibid

Chapter II—Revenue Cutters of 1860

1. *Record of Movements, Vessels of the United States Coast Guard 1790-1935*. Record Group 26, National Archives, Washington, D.C.. Vols 1 and 2
2. Ibid, Vol. 1, pp. 83, 84
3. Ibid
4. Journal of *Andrew Jackson,* Jan. 1, 1861
5. *Record of Movements*. Vol. 2, p. 389
6. *Personal Records Relating to Officers and Cadets, 1833-1915*. Record Group 26, National Archives. Joseph Amazeen
7. *Record of Movements*. Vol. 1, p. 43
8. Ibid. The *San Francisco*, a new steamer with sail, left New York on her maiden voyage December 22, 1953, for San Francisco with 500 artillery men and officers on board. In the Gulf Stream she encountered a hurricane, broached to, and was struck by a wave which swept away the lifeboats and the after-saloon with its cabins. About 140 enlisted men were lost overboard. Four vessels succeeded in rescuing the rest of the enlisted men and 212 others on board before the cutters reached the scene.
9. Ibid
10. Journal of *Morris,* 1860
11. *Record of Movements*. Vol. 1, p. 343
12. Journal of *James Campbell*. Nov. 1860
13. *Record of Movements*. Vol. 1, pp. 35-37
14. Truman R. Strobridge, *The United States Coast Guard and the Civil War*. Washington, D.C., U.S.C.G.. 1972. Preface

15. Paul H. Johnson, *Harriet Lane, Great Ship, Great Lady.* The Bulletin, United States Coast Guard Academy, New London, Conn., Sept.-Oct. 1982

16. Journal of *Harriet Lane,* 1858

17. Ibid, 1860

18. *Letters Received By the Treasury Department 1836-1910 From Collectors, Revenue Cutter Captains and Others.* Record Group 26, National Archives, Washington, D.C., Oct. 22, 1860

19. Journal of *Harriet Lane,* Dec. 1860

20. *Record of Movements,* Vol. 1, pp. 98-104

21. Ibid

22. Ibid

23. Journal of *Walter B. Forward,* Dec. 1860

24. *Record of Movements.* Vol. 2, p. 405

25. Journal of *Philip Allen,* Aug. 5, 1860

26. *Record of Movements.* Vol. 2, p. 415

27. Journal of *William J. Duane,* Dec, 1860

28. *Record of Movements.* Vol. 1, p. 149

29. *Personal Records.* Napoleon L. Coste

30. Journal of *William Aiken,* Dec. 1859

31. *Record of Movements.* Vol. 1, pp. 201-202

32. Journal of *James C. Dobbin,* Dec. 20, 1860

33. *Record of Movements.* Vol. 2, p. 416

34. *Letters Received.* 1860

35. *Record of Movements.* Vol. 2, p. 419

36. Journal of *Lewis Cass.* June-Dec. 1860

37. Journal of *Robert McClelland,* 1854-1859

38. Ibid Dec. 29, 1860

39. *Record of Movements.* Vol. 1, p. 97

40. Howard Chapelle, *The American Sailing Navy.* New York: Bonanza Books, 1920. pp. 374-377

41. Journal of *Washington,* Nov. 27, 1860

42. *Record of Movements.* Vol. 2, p. 390

43. *Personal Records.* Levy. C. Harby

44. Journal of *Henry Dodge,* May 1860

45. Ibid, Nov. 1860

46. *South Carolina Mercury,* Charleston, S.C., Dec. 29, 1860

47. Journal of *Henry Dodge,* Dec. 29, 1860

48. *Record of Movements.* Vol. 2, p. 419 and Vol. 1, p. 67

49. *Contract and Specifications for William Marcy and Jefferson Davis.* Dukes County Historical Society, Edgartown, Mass.

50. *Record of Movements.* Vol. 2, p. 419

51. Ibid, Vol. 2, pp. 395-396

52. *Letters Received.* Apr. 4, 1861

53. Floremce Kern, *Captain Pease, Coast Guard Pioneer.* Bethesda, Md.: Alised Enterprises, 1982, p. 62

54. Journal of *Jefferson Davis,* Dec. 1860

55. Kern, p. 64-67

II

Chapter III—New Flags for Old

1. *Charleston Daily Courier,* Charleston, S.C. Dec. 20, 1860
2. Journal of *William Aiken.* Dec. 27, 1860
3. Ibid
4. Ibid, Dec. 28, 1860
5. Ibid
6. *Personal Records.* Napoleon L. Coste
7. *Charleston Daily Courier.* Dec. 29, 1860
8. *Personal Records.* John Underwood, Henry O. Porter and Horace J. Gambrill
9. Journal of *William Aiken.* Jan. 1, 1861
10. Ibid
11. Journal of *James Dobbin.* Jan. 2, 1861
12. Ibid, Jan. 3, 1861
13. *Letters Received.* Jan. 3, 1861
14. Ibid
15. Ibid
16. Journal of *James Dobbin,* Jan. 3, 1861
17. Journal of *Lewis Cass,* Jan. 30, 1861
18. *Letters Received.* Feb. 1861
19. *Personal Records.* James G. Morrison
20. Strobridge, p. 4
21. *Personal Records.* Anson S. Rogers, Thomas H. Lawrence and Charles G. Shoemaker
22. Journals of *Washington* and *Robert McClelland.* Oct. 24, 1860
23. *Letters Received.* Dec. 1860
24. *Applications For Positions in the Revemue Marine Service 1844-1880.* Record Group 26, National Archives, Washington, D.C. John G. Breshwood
25. Journal of *McClelland,* Dec. 1860
26. Thomas J. Scharf, *History of the Confederate States Navy.* Albany, N.Y.: Joseph McDonagh, 1887. p. 24
27. *Letters Received.* 1863
28. Ibid, Feb. 1861
29. *Personal Records.* John G. Breshwood, Samuel B. Caldwell and Thomas D. Fister
30. Journal of *William Dodge,* Feb. 1861
31. Ibid
32. *Personal Records.* William F. Rogers
33. Journal of *William Duane.* Feb. 18, 1861
34. Ibid
35. *Letters Received.* Apr. 1861
36. Ibid
37. Ibid

Chapter IV—The First Shot

1. Roy P. Basler, editor, *The Collected Works of Abraham Lincoln 1861-1865.* New Brunswick, N.J.: Rutgers University Press, 1952-1955. 8 Vols. Vol. 4, p. 221
2. Jones, Virgil C., *The Civil War at Sea.* New York: Holt, Rinehart and Winston, 1960-1962. Vol. 1, pp. 83-91
3. Ibid

4. *Personal Records.* John McGowan

5. *Applications for Positions.* 1848

6. Ibid

7. Ibid

8. Ibid, 1853

9. Ibid, 1858

10. Jones, Vol. 1, p. 91

11. Ibid

12. Ibid

13. *Letters Received* 1861

14. *Applications.* John McGowan

15. *Personal Records.* John McGowan

16. Journal of *Dobbin.* Apr. 17-18, 1861

17. *Letters Received.* April 20, 1861

18. Journal of Dobbin. Apr. 17-18, 1861

19. *Letters Received.* Apr. 20, 1861

20. Ibid

21. Ibid

22. Journal of Dobbin. Apr.-May 1861

23. *Record of Movements.* Vol. 1, p. 202

24. Journal of *Forward.* Apr. 25, 1861

25. *Letters Received.* 1861

Chapter V—The Navy and the Revenue Marine

1. Basler, Vol. 4, p. 284

2. Ibid, p. 285

3. Ibid

4. Ibid

5. Ibid

6. Journal of *Harriet Lane,* March 6, 1861

7. Ibid, March 28, 1861

8. Charles B. Boynton, *The History of the Navy During the Rebellion.* New York: D. Appleton and Company, 1867, p. 265

9. Ibid

10. *Official Records of the Union and Confederate Navies in the War of the Rebellion.* (ORN) Washington, D.C.: GPO, Series 1, vol. 4, p. 243

11. Ibid, p. 238

12. Basler, vol. 4, p. 366. Lincoln later said he had confused the names of the Navy vessels.

13. ORN Series 1, vol. 4, p. 366

14. Jones, vol. 1, p. 56

15. ORN Series 1, vol. 4, p. 336

16. Basler, Vol. 4, p. 350

17. Ibid, p. 342

18. Ibid, p. 370

Chapter VI—The Rise and Fall of Captain Howard

1. *Letters Sent by the Treasury Department 1790-1897 to Collectors, Revenue Cutter Captains and Others,* Washington, D.C.: National Archives, Record Group 26, Apr. 1861
2. *Personal Records.* William A. Howard
3. *Letters Received.* May 1861
4. Ibid, 1861
5. Ibid
6. Ibid
7. Ibid, May 15-18, 1861
8. Ibid, May 18, 1861
9. Ibid
10. Ibid, June 1861
11. Ibid. Howard had not recommended examining captains.
12. Ibid
13. Ibid
14. Ibid
15. Journal of *Morris.* Sept. 3, 1861
16. Journal of *Jackson.* Sept. 1861
17. *Letters Received.* July 12, 1861
18. Ibid
19. Journal of *Bibb.* May 1861
20. *Letters Sent.* Aug-Oct. 1861
21. Ibid
22. Ibid
23. Ibid
24. Ibid
25. *Letters Received.* July 12, 1861
26. Ibid
27. Ibid. There is no mention of this rendez-vous in the Journal of the *Morris*, and neither she nor *Cushing* went to the Grand Banks and Sable Island. They spent a week in the vicinity of Martha's Vineyard and Nantucket.
28. Ibid
29. Journal of *Jackson.* July 1861
30. Ibid
31. Journal of *Morris.* July 1861
32. *Letters Received.* Aug. 1861
33. Ibid
34. Journal of *Philip Allen.* Oct. 27, 1861
35. *Personal Records.* William A. Howard

Chapter VII—Captain Faunce and the *Harriet Lane*

1. *Journal of Harriet Lane,* 1858-1861
2. *Letters Received.* Sept. 2, 1861
3. Ibid
4. David Dixon Porter, *The Naval History of the Civil War.* New York: Sherman Publishing Company. p. 29
5. *Letters Received.* Apr. 1861

6. *Letters Sent.* Apr. 1861

7. Philip Yanaway. *Harriet Lane.* Salem, Mass.: Peabody Institute, The American Neptune XXXVI, July 1976, p. 174

8. *Orn* Series 1, vol. 5, p. 698

9. Ibid

10. Ibid

11. *Letters Received.* July 1861

12. *Orn* Series 1, vol. 6., p. 95. Some records say that the *Petrel* was the ex-Revenue Cutter *Aiken* with a new name. This is dubious. There was a Coast Survey vessel *Petrel* seized at the same time as *Aiken.* It is more likely that this vessel became the privateer.

13. Ibid, pp. 129-131

14. Ibid

15. Chief Engineer Frank H. Pulsifer, *Under Lincoln.* Washington, D.C.: U.S.C.G., The Coast Guard, vol. 1, No. 4, Feb. 1928, p. 4

16. *Orn* Series 1, vol. 6, pp. 129-131

17. *Letters Sent.* Sept. 1861

18. Ibid

19. *Letters Received.* Sept. 1861

20. Ibid. It is significant that Lincoln referred to the service as the "Revenue Cutter Service", a name not used officially until 1863.

21. Pulsifer, p. 4

22. Ibid

23. Under Commander Wainwright, U.S.N. *Harriet Lane* was captured by the Confederates in 1863 at Galveston and fitted as a privateer. She was renamed *Lavinia.* At the end of the war, she was in Havana. In 1867, Captain Faunce was sent to Havana to bring her back to New York. She was then sold to Elliot Ritchie and renamed *Helena Ritchie.* As a merchant vessel, she sank in a hurricane in the Caribbean.

Chapter VIII—New Problems for the Revenue Marine

1. *Record of Movements.* Vol. 2, p. 405

2. Journal of *Tiger.* Nov. 30-Dec. 20, 1861

3. Ibid, Dec. 1, 1861

4. Ibid, Dec. 4, 1861

5. *Letters Received.* Dec. 1861

6. Journal of *Tiger.* Dec. 5, 1861

7. Ibid, Dec. 10, 1861

8. Ibid, Dec. 13, 1861

9. *Letters Received.* Dec. 20, 1861

10. Journal of *Tiger.* Dec. 1862

11. Ibid, Jan. 1, 1863

12. Ibid, July 1865

13. John S. Parkinson, *History of the New York Yacht Club.* New York: N.Y.Y.C., 1975, p. 44

14. *Letters Sent.* May 6, 1861

15. *Letters Received.* July 12, 1861

16. *Record of Movements.* Vol. 2, p. 422

17. *Orn* Series 1, vol. 2, pp. 432-439

18. Ibid

19. Wilmington, N.C. Journal. Feb. 13, 1862

20. *Orn* Series 1, vol. 2, pp. 432-435

21. Wilmington, N.C. Journal. Feb. 13, 1862

22. *Letters Received.* Apr. 29, 1862

23. Parkinson, p. 49

24. *Letters Received.* Aug. 1861

25. Ibid

26. Ibid

27. Ibid

28. Ibid, Nov. 4, 1862

29. Journal of *Joe Miller.* Sept. 3-11, 1862

30. Journal of *Cruiser.* Sept. 12-30, 1862

31. Ibid

Chapter IX—The Chilly Voyage of Captain Ottinger

1. *Letters Sent.* Oct. 1861

2. Ibid, Aug. 13, 1861

3. Kern, p. 66

4. *Letters Received.* Oct. 6, 1861

5. Ibid

6. Ibid

7. Ibid

8. Ibid, Oct. 22, 1861

9. Ibid

10. Ibid, Oct. 23, 1861

11. Ibid, Dec. 6, 1861

12. Ibid

13. Ibid

14. Journal of *Morris.* Dec. 25, 1861

15. *Record of Movements.* Vol. 2, p. 417

16. *Letters Received.* Dec. 30, 1861

17. Journal of *Morris.* Dec. 25, 1861

18. *Personal Records.* Anson L. Hyde

19. Journal of *Black.* 1862

20. Journal of *Brown.* 1862

21. *Record of Movements.* Vols. 1 and 2

22. *Letters Sent.* Jan. 1862

23. *Letters Received.* March 1862

Chapter X—President Lincoln on Board Cutter *Miami*

1. Nicolay, John G. and Hay, John, *Complete Works of Abraham Lincoln.* New York: Francis D. Tandy Company, 1882. Vol. 7, p. 153

2. Carl Sandburg, *Abraham Lincoln, The War Years.* New York: Harcourt Brace and Company, 1939. 4 vols. Vol. 1, p. 486

3. Journal of *Miami.* 1864. Evans calls her a yacht.

4. *Letters Sent.* Apr. 3, 1861

5. Journal of *Miami.* Jan 1, 1864

6. Ibid, Apr. 10, 1862

7. Ibid, Apr. 12, 1862

8. Ibid, May 1862

9. Ibid, May 5, 1862

10. Ibid

11. Sandburg, pp. 486-488

12. Journal of *Miami*. May 7, 1862

13. Fort Monroe Casement Museum, *Tales of Old Fort Monroe; Abraham Lincoln's Campaign Against the Merrimack.* Box 341, Fort Monroe, Va. No date, pp. 1-4

14. Ibid

15. Journal of *Miami*. May 7, 1862

16. *Tales of Old Fort Monroe.* Pg. 1

17. Journal of *Miami*. May 7, 1862

18. Ibid, May 8, 9, 1862

19. Ibid. *Miami's* officers are said to have asked Lincoln if they should fire on the horsemen. He told them to leave them alone.

20. Ibid, May 10, 1862

21. Ibid

22. Ibid, May 15, 1862

23. Ibid, Sept. 29, 1862

Chapter XI—Cutters on the West Coast

1. Delgado, James P., *In the Midst of a Great Excitement; the Argosy of the Revenue Cutter C. W. Lawrence.* Salem, Mass.: Peabody Museum. The American Neptune, vol. XLV, No. 2, Spring 1985. Pp. 128-129

2. *Record of Movements.* Vol. 1, p. 75

3. Ibid, p. 128

4. Ibid, Vol. 1, pp. 67, 305-306; vol. 2, p. 419

5. Kern, p. 69

6. Ibid, p. 128

7. *Letters and Papers of William Cooke Pease.* Edgartown, Mass: Dukes County Historical Society

8. Journal of *Joseph Lane.* June 1861

9. Ibid, Aug.-Oct. 1861

10. Journal of *Marcy.* Nov. 2, 1861

11. *Civil War Naval Chronology* 1861-1865. Washington, D.C.: Navy Department, Naval History Division, 1971, pp. 61-65

12. *Letters Received.* Nov. 1861

13. Ibid

14. Journal of *Shubrick.* Nov. 13, 1861

15. *Description of Revenue Cutter Shubrick.* Edgartown, Mass.: Dukes County Historical Society

16. *Letters Sent.* March 5, 1862

17. Journal of *Shubrick.* Jan. 1862

18. Ibid, Jan. 18-25, 1862

19. Ibid, Feb. 15, 1862

20. Ibid, Jan.-July 1862

21. *Letters Received.* Apr.-May 1862

22. *Letters Sent.* May 1862

23. Sandburg, vol. 1., p. 232

24. Kern, p. 75
25. Ibid, p. 84
26. Basler, vol. 6, p. 202
27. Hubert Howe Bancroft. *History of the Pacific States of North America.* San Francisco, The History Company, 1890, p. 230
28. Kern, p. 111

Chapter XII—Cushing Captured at Portland, Maine

1. *Letters Received.* Disposition taken at Portland, Maine, June 29, 1863
2. Ibid
3. Herbert C.F. Adams, *The Comedy of the Caleb Cushing.* Reprinted from the Civil War Times. No date.
4. *Letters Received.* Disposition
5. Ibid
6. Adams, p. 32
7. *Letters Received.* July 24, 1863
8. Adams, p. 35
9. *Letters Received.* June 29, 1863
10. Adams, p. 33
11. *Letters Received.* July 1863
12. Adams, pp. 33-35
13. Ibid, p. 33
14. *Letters Received.* July 1863
15. Ibid
16. *Letters Received.* June-July 1863
17. Ibid
18. Ibid
19. Ibid
20. Adams, p. 33
21. Journal of *Dobbin.* Aug. 13, 1863
22. Ibid, Aug. 1863
23. Ibid, 1864
24. Ibid
25. Ibid, Feb-June, 1864
26. Ibid, Jan 1865

Chapter XIII—Sail Bows to Steam

1. *Record of Movements.* Vols. 1 and 2
2. Journals of *Cruiser* and *Joe Miller*
3. *Record of Movements, Vols. 1 and 2*
4. *Orn* Series 2, vol. 1, p. 215
5. *Record of Movements, Vols 1 and 2*
6. Ibid vol. 2, p. 416
7. Ibid
8. William A. Still Jr. *Iron Afloat.* Vanderbilt University Press, 1971, p. 485
9. Harper's Weekly, July-Dec. 1862, p. 585
10. *Letters Received.* May 28, 1862

11. *Letters Sent.* March 12, 1861

12. Ibid, Apr. 1, 1861

13. *Personal Records.* D.C. Constable

14. *Orn* Series 1, vol. 7., pp. 215-222

15. Journal of *Stevens.* July 1863

16. *Personal Records.* D.C. Constable

17. Journal of *Stevens.* July 1863

18. *Letters Sent.* Dec. 13, 1863

19. Journal of *Stevens,* July 1863, and *Record of Movements,* vol. 1, p. 329

Chapter XIV—More New Revenue Cutters

1. Basler, vol. 7, p. 190

2. *Record of Movements,* vol. 2, p. 390

3. Journal of *Cuyahoga.* July 1863

4. Ibid, 1863-1865

5. Pulsifer, p. 5

6. *Record of Movements.* Vol. 2, p. 390

7. Ibid, p. 75

8. Journal of *Pawtuxet.* 1863-1866

9. *Record of Movements.* Vol. 2, p. 415

10. Ibid, vol. 1, p. 75

11. Journal of *Ashuelot.* 1863-1864

12. *Record of Movements,* vol. 1, p. 75

13. Ibid, pp. 290-294

14. Journal of *Mahoning.* 1863-1865

15. *Record of Movements,* vol. 1, p. 294

16. Ibid, p. 172

17. Journal of *Wayanda.* 1863-1866

18. *Record of Movements.* Vol. 2, p. 1722

19. *Letters Received.* Sept. 15, 1863

20. Ibid, Feb. 5, 1865

21. *Record of Movements.* Vol. 2, p. 416

22. Ibid, p. 417

23. Journal of *Kewanee,* Aug. 1864 and Vineyard Gazette Edgartown, Mass.: Aug. 1864

24. Ibid, 1863-1864

25. *Record of Movements.* Vol. 2. p. 424

26. Ibid, p. 424

Chapter XV—Cutters in Combat in 1864

1. *Record of Movements.* Vol. 2, p. 418

2. Journal of *Nemaha.* June 1864

3. Ibid, 1864-1865

4. Ibid, Dec. 1, 1864

5. Ibid, Dec. 1864

6. Ibid, Jan. 1, 1865

7. Ibid, Feb.-June 1865

8. *Record of Movements.* Vol. 2, p. 418

9. Journal of *Reliance*. Aug. 12, 1864
10. Ibid, 1863-1864
11. *Letters Received*. 1864
12. Journal of *Reliance*. 1864
13. Ibid, Aug. 12, 1864

Chapter XVI—The Four Great Captains

1. *Personal Records*. Howard, Faunce, McGowan, Ottinger
2. *Letters Received*. June 25, 1863
3. Ibid, 1864
4. *Letters Sent*. 1864
5. Ibid
6. *Record of Movements*. Vol 2, p. 67
7. Journal of *Antietam*, 1864-1871
8. *Record of Movements*. Vol. 1, p. 67
9. Ibid, pp. 216-220
10. Journal of *Northerner*. Apr. 19, 1865
11. Ibid, 1865-1866
12. *Record of Movements*. Vol. 1, p. 220
13. Ibid, p. 270-273
14. Ibid, p. 273
15. *Annual Report of the American Historical Society*, 1896. Washington, D.C.: G.P.O. 1897. Vol. 1, pp. 344-349
16. *Letters Received*. Oct. 18, 1864
17. Ibid
18. Ibid, Dec. 1864

The Revenue Cutters in the Civil War

Selective Bibliography

Records

Record of Movements: Vessels of the United States Coast Guard 1790-Dec. 31, 1933, Volumes 1 and 2. Compiled in the office of the Assistant Commandant, U.S. Coast Guard, U.S. Coast Guard Headquarters, Washington, D.C., 1933. Issued by the Treasury Department Feb. 15, 1935.

Record Group 26, National Archives. Records of the Revenue Cutters of the United States Coast Guard:

Applications for Positions in the Revenue Cutter Service 1831-1871

Personal Records Relating to Officers and Cadets 1833-1915

Correspondence & Specifications relating to the construction and repairs of revenue cutters 1845-1910

Muster Rolls 1843-1914

Letters sent by the Treasury Department 1790-1882 and 1871-1897 to Collectors, Revenue Cutter Captains and others. 212 volumes.

Letters received by the Treasury Department 1836-1910 from Collectors, Revenue Cutter Captains and Others. 308 vols.

Letters from Collectors to the Treasury Department on Revenue Cutter activities 1834-1853

Letters from Officers of Cutters to the Treasury Department 1833-1869. (By name of vessel and then chronologically)

Miscellaneous correspondence 1793-1937 (By name of station and vessel, then chronologically)

History of Revenue Cutters 1790-1937. Thirteen volumes — Record of claims

Examinations for the Revenue Marine (Cutter) Service 1861-1892

Applications for the Revenue Marine (Cutter) Service 1844-1880

Ships Rosters 1819-1904

List of logs (journals) of U.S. Coast Guard vessels 1790-1941 as compiled by Thornton W. Mitchell and Arthur Dyer of the Division of Treasury Dept. Archives and presented by U.S.C.G. in 1944. The list has been updated by National Archives staff and Coast Guard historians. (n.b. This list also contains the names of cutters for which no logs (journals) have been found, as noted below, and identifies the periods for which logs (journals) of others are missing. Cutters of the Civil War period and their years of service are listed as follows:

Agassiz 1861-1866
Aiken, William (Eclipse) 1855-1861
Allen, Philip 1855-1865
Antietam 1864-1869
Appleton, John 1857-1861 (no journals)
Arago 1861 (no journals)
Ashuelot 1863-1867

Bibb 1845-1861
Black, Jeremiah S. 1857-1864
Bronx (Addison Andrews) 1863-1873
Brown, Aaron 1857-1864
Campbell, James 1853-1875
Cass, Lewis 1856-1861
Chase, Samuel P. 1865-1875
Cobb, Howell 1857-1861
Commodore Perry 1864-1883
Corwin, Thomas 1861 (no journals)
Crawford 1861-1869
Cushing, Caleb 1853-1863
Cuyahoga (Santa Anna) 1863-1867
Davis, Jefferson 1853-1861
Delaware 1865-1873
Dobbin, James C. 1853-1881
Dodge, Henry 1856-1861
Duane, William J. 1849-1861
Fessenden, William P. 1865-1908
Forward, Walter 1842-1865
Hector 1864
Henrietta 1861-1862 (no journals)
Hercules 1861-1864
Hope 1861
Jackson, Andrew 1833-1865
Johnson, Andrew 1865-1897
Kankakee 1863-1867
Kewanee 1863-1867
Lane, Harriet 1857-1861
Lane, Joseph (Campbell) 1849-1869
Lincoln, 1864-1874
McClelland, Robert 1853-1861
McCulloch, Hugh 1865-1876
Mahoning (Levi Woodbury) 1863-1873
Marcy, William L. 1853-1862
Miami (Lady Le Marchant) 1862-1871
Miller, Joe 1862
Mocassin 1865-1891
Morris 1849-1868
Nansemond 1865-1873
Nemaha (Flora) 1862-1868
Northerner (Ewing) 1864-1874
Pawtuxet 1864-1867
Reliance 1861-1865
Seward, William H. 1864-1901
Shubrick, William 1856-1867
Stevens, E.A. (Naugatuck) 1861-1889
Sumner, General 1861 (no journals)
Thompson, Jacob 1857-1869
Tiger 1861-1865
Toucey, Isaac 1857-1869
Uno 1865-1873
Varina 1861-1865
Vixen 1861 (no journals)
Wayanda (Wawayanda) 1863-1878

Wilderness 1865-1873
Winslow 1864 (no journals)
Zoave 1861 (no journals; yacht not commissioned)

Record Group 23, National Archives. Records of the Coast and Geodetic Survey.

Record Group 41, National Archives. Records of the Bureau of Marine Inspection.

Record Group 36, National Archives. Treasury Department. Letters to and from Collectors and Special Agents.

Record Group 56, National Archives. General records of the Department of the Treasury with data on the revenue marine and lighthouses.

Record Group 45, National Archives. Subject file of the Confederate Navy 1861-1865.

Office Records of the Union and Confederate Navies in the War of the Rebellion. Washington, D.C. General Printing Office 1874.

Dictionary of American Naval Fighting Ships. Washington, D.C.: Navy Department, Naval History Division. 1963.

United States Revenue Marine Register: 1873-1875. Dukes Country Historical Society, Edgartown, Mass. New York: The Nautical History Press 1873-1875.

Merchant Steam Vessels of the United States 1790-1868. The Lytle-Holdcamper List edited and compiled by C. Bradford Mitchell and Kenneth R. Hall. Staten Island, New York: The Steamship Historical Society of New York. 1975.

Whalemen's Shipping List and Merchants' Transcripts. New Bedford, Mass. 1863.

Civil War Naval Chronology 1861-1865. Washington, D.C.: Navy Department, Naval History Division. 1971.

Guide to Federal Archives Relating to the Civil War. Washington, D.C.: General Printing Office.

Congressional Record 12 Stat. 639, Feb. 4, 1863.

Books

Anderson, Bern, *By Sea and River,* The Naval History of the Civil War. New York: Alfred Knopf, 1902.

Annual Report of the American Historical Society, Vol. 1. Washington, D.C.: G.P.O. 1897.

Baarsley, Karl, *Coast Guard to the Rescue,* New York and Toronto: Farrar and Rinehart, 1936.

Bancroft, Hubert Howe, *History of the Pacific States of North America.* San Francisco: The History Company, 1890.

Barnes, James, *Photographic History of the Civil War.* New York: Review of Reviews, 1911.

Basler, Roy P., editor, *The Collected Works of Abraham Lincoln* 1861-1865. New Brunswick, N.J.: Rutgers University Press, 1963, 8 Vols.

Battles and Leaders of the Civil War. Grant-Lee Edition, Vols. 1 & 2. New York: Century Company, 1884-1887.

Beale, Roy P., editor, *Diary of Gideon Welles.* New York: W.W. Norton, 1960.

Bennett, Frank M., *Steam Navy of the United States.* Pittsburgh, Pa: Press of W.T. Nicholson, 1898.

Benson, J. Lossing, *A History of the Civil War.* New York: War Memorial Association, 1912.

Bloomfield, Howard V.L., *The Compact History of the United States Coast Guard.* New York: Hawthorne Books, 1966.

Boatner, Mark Mayo, *The Civil War Dictionary.* New York: David McKay Company, 1939.

Boynton, Charles B. *History of the Navy During the Rebellion.* New York: D. Appleton Company, 1867.

Cajori, Florian, *The Chequered Career of Ferdinand Rudolph Hassler, First Superintendent of the Coast and Geodetic Survey.* Baltimore: The Johns Hopkins Press, 1923.

Catton, Bruce, *Never Call Retreat,* The Centennial History of the Civil War, Vol. 3. Garden City, New York: Doubleday and Company, 1965.

Charleston Year Book, Charleston, S.C., 1884.

Chapelle, Howard, *The American Sailing Navy.* New York: Bonanza Books, 1920.

Comte de Paris, *History of the Civil War in America.* Philadelphia: Porter and Coates, 1875.

Cooper, Reverend W.H., *Incidents of Shipwrecks, or the Loss of the San Francisco.* Philadelphia, 1855.

Dufour, Charles L., *The Night the War Was Lost.* New York: Doubleday and Company Inc., 1960.

Dyer, Frederick H., *A Compendium of the War of the Rebellion.* Des Moines, Iowa: 1908.

Encyclopedia Americana. Danbury, Conn.: Grolier Inc., 1984

Evans, Captain Stephens H., U.S.C.G., *United States Coast Guard: A Definitive History.* Annapolis, Maryland: Naval Institute, 1939.

Foote, Shelby, *The Civil War.* New York: Random House, 1963.

Guernsey, Alfred H., and Pease, Alden Fairfax, *Harpers Pictorial History of the Civil War.* New York: Fairfax Press, 1966.

Hawkes, Esther Hill, *Diary, A Woman Doctor's Civil War,* edited by Gerald Schwartz. University of South Carolina Press, 1984.

Hughes, Riley, *Our Coast Guard Academy.* New York: Devin-Adair Company, 1929.

Jones, Virgil C., *The Civil War at Sea.* 3 vol. New York, Holt, Rinehart, Winston Company, 1960-1962.

Kaplan, Hyman R., *The U.S. Coast Guard and The Civil War,* Cornell Maritime Press, 1971.

Kaplan, Hyman R., *The U.S. Coast Guard and The Civil War.* Washington, D.C.: General Printing Office, 1961.

Kern, Florence, Captain Pease, U.S. Coast Guard Pioneer. Bethesda, Md.: Alised Enterprises, 1982

Kerr, Evan Samuel Jr., *The United States Guard, Its Ships, Duties, Stations,* New York, Robert W. Kelly Publishing Corporation, 1935

Long, Everette B., *The Civil War Day by Day.* New York: Doubleday and Company, 1971

Mahan, Alfred T., *The Navy in The Civil War.* New York: Charles Scribner's Sons, 1895

Miers, Earl Schanck, *Lincoln Day by Day.* Washington, D.C.: Lincoln Sesquicentennial, 1960

Miller, Francis Trevelyan, editor, *Photographic History of The Civil War.* Springfield, Mass.: Review of Reviews Company, 1911

Moore, Frank, editor, *Rebellion Record,* 1860-1861. New York: G. P. Putnam, 1862.

Nash, Howard P. Jr., *A Naval History of The Civil War.* A. S. Barnes and Company Inc., 1972.

Newell, G. R., *Ships of the Inland Sea, The Story of the Puget Sound Steamboats,* 1951.

Nicolay, John G. and Hay, John, editors, *Complete Works of Abraham Lincoln,* New York, Francis D. Tandy Company. 1882. 10 Vols.

Osbon, B. S., *Handbook of the U. S. Navy.* New York: D. Van Nostrand, 1864

Parkinson, John J., *History of the New York Yacht Club.* New York: New York Yacht Club, 1975.

Porter, David Dixon, *The Naval History of The Civil War.* New York: The Sherman Publishing Company, 1886.

Robertson, James Jr., editor, *Index Guide to the Southern Historical Society Papers* 1876-1959. 2 vols. Millwood, New York: Kraus International Publishing Company. Reprint, Barre, Vt., 1960

Robinson, Thomas Morrison Jr. *The Confederate Privateers.* New Haven : Yale University Press, 1928.

Sandburg, Carl, *Abraham Lincoln, The War Years,* 4 volumes. New York: Harcourt Brace and Company, 1939.

Scharf, J. Thomas, *History of the Confederate States Navy.* Albany, New York: Joseph McDonagh, 1894.

Smith, Horatio Davis, *Early History of the United States Revenue Marine Service,* edited by Elliott Snow USN Ret. Washington D.C., 1932.

Snowden, Yates, *History of South Carolina.* Chicago-New York: Lewis Publishing company, 1920.

Still, William N. Jr., *The Story of the Confederate Ironclads.* Vanderbilt University Press, 1971.

Swanberg, W.A., *First Blood, The Story of Fort Sumter.* New York: Charles Scribner's Sons, 1957.

Tilp, Frederic. *This was Potomac River.* Alexandria, Va.:1978

Wakelyn, John L., editor, *Biographical Dictionary of the Confederacy.* Westport, Conn. and London: Greenwood Press, 1977.

Weber, Gustavus Adolphus, *The Coast and Geodetic Survey.* Baltimore: Johns Hopkins Press, 1923.

West, Richard S. Jr., *Mr. Lincoln's Navy.* Westport, Conn.: Greenwood Press, 1957.

Wilson, John Laird, *Pictorial History of the Great Civil War.* New York City, 1878

Manuscripts

Steere, Emily, *Martha's Vineyard During The Civil War.* Dukes County Historical Society, Edgartown, Mass.: 1960

Stone, Charles Henry, *Cruise of the U. S. Navy Steamer Harriet Lane, 1863.* Typewritten copy of manuscript in United States Coast Guard Academy, New London, Conn.

Easby, Wilhemina M., *Personal Recollections of Early Washington, and a Sketch of the Life of Captain William Easby.* A paper read before the Association of Oldest Inhabitants of the District of Columbia, June 4, 1913. Columbia Museum, Washington, D.C.

Pamphlets and Articles

Johnson, Paul H., *Harriet Lane, Great Ship, Great Lady.* The Bulletin, United States Coast Guard Academy, Sept.-Oct 1982. Vol. 44

Adams, C.F., *The Comedy of the Caleb Cushing.* Reprinted from The Civil War Times. No date given.

Fort Monroe Casement Museum, *Tales of Old Fort Monroe, #9. Abraham Lincoln.* No date or author given.

Lighthouses and Lightships of the Northern Gulf of Mexico. USCG. No date or author given.

U.S. Coast Guard and The Civil War. USCG. 1972. No author given.

The United States Revenue Marine; Its Cutters and Semper Paratus. USCG. No date or author given.

United States Coast Guard: Activities Afloat and Ashore. USCG, Tide Rips, 1934

Strobridge, Truman, *Annotated Bibliography of the United States Coast Guard.* Department of Transportation, 1972

Strobridge, Truman, *The United States Coast Guard and The Civil War,* Washington, D.C., United States Coast Guard, Public Affairs Division, 1972

Survey of a Portion of Ocean Beach, San Francisco, for the Revenue Cutter C. W. Lawrence. U.S. Department of the Interior, National Park Service, Golden Gate National Recreation Area, 1984

Yanaway, Philip E., *Harriet Lane.* American Neptune, July 1976

Delgado, James P., *In the Midst of a Great Excitement; The Argosy of the Revenue Cutter C. W. Lawrence;* The American Neptune Vol. XLV No.2, Peabody Museum, Salem, Mass.1985

XVI

Pulsifer, F.H., *Reminisences of the Harriet Lane,* Journal of the United States Coast Guard Academy, 1917; *Under Lincoln,* The Coast Guard,Vol.1,No. 4,U.S. Coast Guard, Washington,D.C.Feb.1928

Newspapers and Magazines

The Bulletin, United States Coast Guard Academy, New London, Conn.
Century Magazine
Charleston Daily Courier
Civil War Times
Harpers Weekly
New Orleans Daily True Delta
New York Tribune
South Carolina Mercury
Vineyard Gazette, Edgartown, Mass.

Index

XX

www.ingramcontent.com/pod-product-compliance
Lightning Source LLC
Chambersburg PA
CBHW060652150426
42813CB00052B/723